MW01487537

# Memorizing Scripture: Why Bother?

## A Method Enriched by Heartfelt Stories and Reflections

## Herb Ruby

STORIED
publishing
editing
coaching
storied.pub

Copyright © 2023 Herb Ruby

All rights reserved.

No part of this book may be reproduced in any form or by any electronic or mechanical means, including information storage and retrieval systems, without written permission from the author, except for the use of brief quotations in a book review.

Bible Translations Used:

New International Version, 1978 Edition

New American Standard Bible, 1973

New King James Version, 1982

ISBN: 978-1-951991-36-4

Edited and typeset by Doug Serven

Cover design by Sean Benesh

Cover art by Shelley Ruby

Published by Storied Publishing

# Contents

Praise for Memorizing Scripture: Why Bother?          vii
Acknowledgments                                      xiii
Why Bother Memorizing Scripture?                       xv
A Personal Note from the Author                       xix

PART ONE
ENCOURAGEMENT

1. Encouragement          3
2. A                      8
3. B                     10
4. C                     12
5. D                     14
6. E                     16
7. F                     18
8. G                     20
9. H                     22
10. I                    24
11. J                    26
12. K                    28
13. L                    30
14. M                    32
15. N                    34
16. O                    36
17. P                    38
18. Q                    40
19. R                    42
20. S                    44
21. T                    46
22. U                    48
23. V                    50
24. W                    52

25. X                                         54
26. Y                                         56
27. Z                                         58

PART TWO
FAITH

28. Faith                                    63
29. A                                        68
30. B                                      70
31. C                                      72
32. D                                      74
33. E                                      76
34. F                                      78
35. G                                    80
36. H                                    82
37. I                                     84
38. J                                    86
39. K                                  88
40. L                                  90
41. M                                  92
42. N                                  94
43. O                                  96
44. P                                  98
45. Q                               100
46. R                               102
47. S                               104
48. T                               106
49. U                               108
50. V                               110
51. W                              112
52. X                               114
53. Y                               116
54. Z                               118

## Part Three
## Witnessing

55. Witnessing      123
56. A      128
57. B      130
58. C      132
59. D      134
60. E      136
61. F      138
62. G      140
63. H      142
64. I      144
65. J      146
66. K      148
67. L      150
68. M      152
69. N      154
70. O      156
71. P      158
72. Q      160
73. R      162
74. S      164
75. T      166
76. U      168
77. V      170
78. W      172
79. X      174
80. Y      176
81. Z      178

## Part Four
## Worship

82. Worship      183
83. A      187
84. B      189
85. C      191

86. D ........................................ 193
87. E ........................................ 195
88. F ........................................ 197
89. G ........................................ 199
90. H ........................................ 201
91. I ........................................ 203
92. J ........................................ 205
93. K ........................................ 207
94. L ........................................ 209
95. M ........................................ 211
96. N ........................................ 213
97. O ........................................ 215
98. P ........................................ 217
99. Q ........................................ 219
100. R ....................................... 221
101. S ....................................... 223
102. T ....................................... 225
103. U ....................................... 227
104. V ....................................... 229
105. W ....................................... 231
106. X ....................................... 233
107. Y ....................................... 235
108. Z ....................................... 237

Appendix A ............................... 239
Appendix B ............................... 253
Appendix C ............................... 255

About the Author ...................... 269

# Praise for Memorizing Scripture: Why Bother?

Herb is my pastor, mentor, and friend. Through stories reflecting on his forty years of ministry to the church he planted, Herb opens the scriptures that have sustained and guided him at every turn. Anyone who knows Herb cannot but hear his pastoral heart in these words. And any who heed his call to commit the scriptures to memory will doubtlessly be blessed. I heartily recommend this book to all who long to know and love God's Word.

**Mark Samuel**

Senior Pastor, Covenant of Grace Presbyterian Church (PCA)

Here is a practical plan that exposes you to key verses in the Bible that will build your inner spiritual core. Herb Ruby's warmth in sharing his heart as well as his knowledge makes memorizing scripture seem not only achievable but thoroughly worthwhile.

With Herb as your spiritual coach, you will benefit from his personal stories and his long experience in providing spiritual guidance and counsel to people in all types of life circumstances. Best of all, you will embed life-changing spiritual truth in your heart.

**Frank Boswell**

Pastor Emeritus, Hunt Valley Church

*Memorizing Scripture: Why Bother?* offers real motivation to internalize God's Word. The personal reflections and applications to life experiences comes from the heart of one of God's genuinely good shepherds. For 39 years, Herb Ruby faithfully reminded his Covenant of Grace flock of the promises of God and shepherded them through the trials and triumphs of life. My life has been enriched by listening to his sermons week after week. I have come to know and trust this shepherd's voice. This book is yet another expression of his desire for people to experience the powerful living benefits of knowing scripture.

**Robert K. Gehman**
President Emeritus, Helping Up Mission


Woven throughout *Memorizing Scripture: Why Bother?* is the accumulated wisdom of a beloved pastor who faithfully served one congregation for his entire career, almost unheard of in our time. The chosen verses in the areas of encouragement, faith, witnessing, and worship bring forth the fullness of God's love and faithfulness to his children. Anyone who commits them to memory will have a strong foundation to rest upon.

The personal reflections and stories are a true gem for anyone who reads the book, and they will encourage you to not only further praise and trust God in all areas of life but will increase your desire to share the good news with family and friends outside the faith. Since Herb came to faith later in life, much of his imparted wisdom relates well to our time when people are leaving the faith. This book could be a great gift to someone who is struggling to find their place in this world that God created.

**Steve Ball**
Senior Vice-president, Gross, Mendelsohn & Assoc. Accounting Firm and PCA Ruling Elder


I have been honored to know Herb Ruby over the four decades he served as pastor of Covenant of Grace and before while being in seminary together. Reading *Memorizing Scripture: Why Bother?* was like being invited to a great feast prepared by a dear friend who served four magnificent courses—Encouragement, Faith, Witnessing, and Worship—packed with so many delightful flavors of personal memoirs and seasonings of biblical insights that it takes the entire alphabet to describe over and over again.

But this banquet is designed not just to be savored but to equip. The guests are invited into God's culinary school of scripture memory in order to become master chefs themselves. *"Oh, taste and see that the LORD is good!"* Read, memorize, and be transformed.

**Craig Garriott**
Pastor Emeritus, Faith Christian Fellowship
Executive Director, Baltimore Antioch Leadership Movement

*This book is dedicated to the members of Covenant of Grace Presbyterian Church (PCA), who, for over thirty-nine years, have listened to and encouraged me in my preaching and teaching of God's Word.*

# Acknowledgments

To Pete Lester, my friend and fellow music team member who first encouraged me to write a book.

To Session members Steve Ball, Jim Beachley, Greg Hard, Ken Harris, Tom Metzbower, Matt Sherlock. Mike Smelser, Bob Wissinger, and my successor, Pastor Mark Samuel—for all your support and encouragement of my preaching, teaching, and leadership at Covenant of Grace.

To my friend Ken Harris, whose endless hours of computer and word processing support have been invaluable.

And above all, to my wife, Shelley, who has been my partner in ministry for over forty-four years. Words are inadequate to express my appreciation for who you are and what you mean to me. Not only are you my cherished wife and mother to our three sons but my #1 cheerleader, encourager, best critic, helper, and most trusted advisor. Your help in editing the content of this book is a tribute to your skill as a superb communicator as well as a skilled critic of my writing skills. Thank you for all you have done to make this book possible.

# WHY BOTHER
# MEMORIZING
# SCRIPTURE?

For most of us, memorizing anything takes commitment, hard work and constant practice. So, the title of this book asks the obvious question, why bother? While memorizing Scripture may be hard, the answer to the question is not. God uses Scripture to change our lives and to guide us into the way that pleases Him. To know God, to love God, and to obey God, you need to know His Word. And while we can carry a phone around with us that has God's Word on it, being able to have God's Word in our heart and on the tip of our tongues for any occasion, gives us confidence and power.

## HOW THIS BOOK MAY BE USED

You can utilize this book in several ways. One may simply want to read through it like a daily devotional. It is set up with that format. But it is uniquely designed to encourage the memorization of verses through the well-documented method of connections.

A University of North Carolina article[1] that is given to freshmen as they begin their studies documents the fact that the more ways you can connect something to what you know, the easier it is to remember. Therefore, this book is designed to give the reader five connections to aid in memorizing Scripture.

The Five Connections for More Effective Memorization are:

1. Four sets of 26 memory verses grouped into **Categories**: They are: Encouragement, Faith, Witnessing, and Worship
2. One **Key Word** in each sentence
3. **Alphabetical** listing of the key words
4. **Understanding** of the verse through a brief illustration and commentary
5. **Application** of the verse through a personal prayer

## THE CHOICE OF TRANSLATION

There are numerous translations of the Bible available, but it is best to pick only one translation for memorization and stick with it. According to Thom S. Rainer, CEO of Church Answers, in 2020 the NIV was the bestselling Bible translation in the USA. To quote Chip Brown, Zondervan's Senior Vice President and Publisher for Bibles, "Since its debut in 1978, the NIV has become and remains the world's bestselling Bible, by God's grace and because the NIV translation philosophy uniquely translates directly from the Bible language into the way English is spoken today."

All of the verses in this book are from the NIV 1978 edition, except where noted. It is the translation this author has personally used for over four decades of ministry.

If another non-paraphrase version is preferred, I would suggest you handwrite over the verse with the translation you wish to use in its place. Such a change may or may not alter the key word and alphabetical order, but should not alter the category, meaning, or application.

## USING THE THREE APPENDICES

Appendix A is designed to help with memorizing after all 104 verses have been learned. Listing four verses having the first letter of the key word together (such as all the A key words) is a sixth method of connections that can aid in memorizing.

Appendix B is a list of well-tested tips for effective memorizing. Different methods work better for different learning styles and circumstances.

Appendix C has been placed in the book as a tool for self-testing. It is recommended that Appendix C be photocopied and used for practice. The alphabetical key word plus several active words have been added as an aid in memorizing.

---

1. UNC Memoraiztion Techniques, https://learningcenter.unc.edu/tips-and-tools/enhancing-your-memory/.

# A PERSONAL NOTE FROM THE AUTHOR

Although memorizing Scripture may be a noble goal in itself, the real motive for memorizing Scripture should be, as the psalmist says, that God's Word *"be hidden in our heart."* To know God's Word by memory means you do not have to open a Bible to know God's will, truth, or His desire for your life. Having God's Word memorized means that His Word is so ingrained in your mind and heart that you can act immediately to whatever circumstance comes.

Knowing, in your heart, the 104 verses included in this book is intended to give you power, strength, and boldness, as well as joy.

Memorizing Scripture will enrich your life in ways too numerous to count. My prayer for you is that in knowing these great verses that you may, *"Grow in the grace and knowledge of our Lord and Savior Jesus Christ"* (2 Peter 3:18).

One final note: please understand that a majority of the illustrations in this book come from my own personal experience. To some degree, this book is autobiographical and contains real-life stories of my and my family's journey of faith.

To God be the glory.

# A PERSONAL NOTE FROM THE AUTHOR

# PART ONE
# ENCOURAGEMENT

# ENCOURAGEMENT

*For everything that was written in the past*
*was written to teach us, so that through endurance and*
*the encouragement of the Scriptures we might have hope.*

—Romans 15:4

## List of Encouragement Verses

"**All** Scripture is God-breathed and is useful for teaching, rebuking, correcting and training in righteousness.
2 Timothy 3:16

"**But** grow in the grace and knowledge of our Lord and Savior Jesus Christ."
2 Peter 3:18

"**Cast** all your anxiety on him because he cares for you. "
1 Peter 5:7

"**Delight** yourself in the LORD and he will give you the desires of your heart."
Psalm 37:4

"**Encourage** one another daily, as long as it is called Today."
Hebrews 3:13

"**For** I know the plans I have for you, declares the LORD, plans to prosper you and not to harm you, plans to give you hope and a future."
Jeremiah 29:11

"**God** is our refuge and strength, an ever-present help in trouble."
Psalm 46:1

"**He** himself is our peace."
Ephesians 2:14

"**I** tell you the truth, he who believes has everlasting life."
John 6:47

"The **joy** of the LORD is your strength."
Nehemiah 8:10

"And we **know** that in all things God works for the good of those who love him, who have been called according to his purpose."
Romans 8:28

"**Love** the Lord your God with all your heart and with all your soul and with all your mind and with all your strength."
Mark 12:30

"**My** grace is sufficient for you, for my power is made perfect in weakness."
Corinthians 12:9

"**Now** that you know these things, you will be blessed if you do them."
John 13:17

"To **obey** is better than sacrifice."
1 Samuel 15:22

"The **plans** of the LORD stand firm forever, the purposes of his heart through all generations."
Psalm 33:11

"Everyone should be **quick** to listen, slow to speak and slow to become angry."
James 1:19

"**Rejoice** in the Lord always. I will say it again: Rejoice! Let your gentleness be evident to all. The Lord is near."
Philippians 4:4

"**Seek** first his kingdom and his righteousness, and all these things will be given to you as well."
Matthew 6:33

"**Therefore**, go and make disciples of all nations, baptizing them in the name of the Father and of the Son and of the Holy Spirit, and teaching them to obey everything I have commanded you."
Matthew 28:19-20

"**Unless** the LORD builds the house, its builders labor in vain."
Psalm 127:1

"This is the **verdict**: light has come into the world. "
John 3:19

"**Work** out your salvation with fear and trembling, for it is God who works in you to will and to act according to his good purpose."
Philippians 2:12-13

"Righteousness **e (x)alts** a nation, but sin is a disgrace to any people."
Proverbs 14:34

"**You** will seek me and find me when you seek me with all your heart."
Jeremiah 29:13

"It is not good to have **<u>zeal</u>** without knowledge."
Proverbs 19:2

# A

*__All__ Scripture is God-breathed and is useful for teaching, rebuking, correcting and training in righteousness.*
2 Timothy 3:16

As you begin reading this book and memorizing the verses, it is important for you to know that I absolutely believe what 2 Timothy 3:16 says. The Bible is the inspired Word of God. Its words are "breathed-out" by God and accurately reveal His character and will.

I did not always believe this. My childhood church did not hold to the view that the Bible was fully inspired. When I went off to a liberal arts college that required two semesters of Bible, the viewpoint of the professor was that it was written by man. The course itself was focused on showing us that the Bible was not trustworthy. As a result of those classes, I became a hardened Bible skeptic and a borderline agnostic.

That all changed at age 28 when I accepted Jesus as my

personal Lord and Savior. Immediately I began reading the Bible for myself and sought to find alternate answers to the skepticism about the Bible I had been taught.

When I read Jesus' words in Matthew 5:18, *"I tell you the truth, until heaven and earth disappear, not the smallest letter, not the least stroke of a pen, will by any means disappear from the Law until everything is accomplished,"* I had the answer I was looking for. Because Jesus affirmed the reliability of the Bible, I did, too.

After studying, teaching, and preaching the Bible as the fully trustworthy Word of God for over four decades, my view has not changed. God has given us in His Word all we need to know Him and please Him. And memorizing and applying the verses contained in this book will greatly bless your life.

**PRAYER**: Dear Lord, as I begin the process of memorizing these verses of Your Word, be with me to encourage me, teach me, and strengthen me so that in knowing these verses by heart, I will know You more.

# B

*<u>**But**</u> grow in the grace and knowledge*
*of our Lord and Savior Jesus Christ.*
2 Peter 3:18

As a mission church starting out from a core group from our mother church, we were looking for an emblem or small piece of artwork that could be used to picture what we wanted to be as a church. One of our artistic members came up with a drawing of a small tree sitting on top of an open Bible. It was just what we needed. Trees grow through the nourishment they receive through their roots planted in good soil. We thought this picture clearly depicted that, as a church, we wanted to grow in Christ by being deeply rooted in the Word of God, the Bible.

There are many verses in the Bible that encourage us to grow through the study and knowledge we receive from God's Word. But there is none so direct and forceful as what we find here. Peter exhorts the believers to whom he is writing to be actively involved in pursuing God's gifts through faith (grace). He also strongly encourages putting effort into the study of God's attributes and will (knowledge). God has revealed in Scripture what we need to know about Him and how to please Him (2 Timothy 3:16).

**PRAYER:** Gracious Lord, may my heart's desire be to know You more. Through knowing Your Word and memorizing it, may I grow in true knowledge of You. May my growth in grace and knowledge bring You glory and praise.

# C

***Cast*** *all your anxiety on him*
*because he cares for you.*
1 Peter 5:7

We had just completed a wonderful Thanksgiving Dinner when the phone rang. It was a call from my wife's doctor with the result of her breast biopsy. Shelley was surprised by the doctor's glibness as she said, "O you have cancer. It's a type that is not supposed to spread. And if you need a surgeon, I can recommend one. Have a happy Thanksgiving. Good-bye". And she hung up.

You can only imagine what we were feeling. Her surgeon had made light of a lump my wife had discovered a year before. Now we had to deal with a disease that had taken the lives of many women we had known.

After we got over the original shock, we prayed. We knew that God had Shelley's life in His hands and the most important thing to do was to turn all our anxiety to Him.

After several surgeries, radiation treatments, and hormone

therapy, a PET scan showed that Shelley was cancer-free. It was a moment of great rejoicing and thanks to God. Now eleven years later, she is still cancer-free. But through that ordeal, we took our anxious thoughts and fears to a God we know cares for us.

**PRAYER:** Lord Jesus, I know that in this life there will be trouble. When it comes, give me the faith to believe that You are concerned with the anxious moments of my life. Help me to know that You care and will be there to comfort and assure me.

# D

*__Delight__ yourself in the LORD and he*
*will give you the desires of your heart.*
Psalm 37:4

I believe this verse should be understood more as a principle than as a promise. My wife and I tried to apply Proverbs 22:6 in raising our sons. We are so thankful how we have been blessed with three men who are professing believers in Jesus Christ and are loving husbands and dads.

One of the things we desired for our sons was wives who loved them and also loved the Lord. We prayed for this for years, and God graciously granted our prayers by giving them wonderfully loving wives, Rani, Heather, and Sandra, who shared their faith.

But this verse is not some formula on how to get whatever you want from God. We all have hopes, dreams, and desires. There are things we love to do and ambitions we would like to fulfill. But sometimes, the things we want to do are not at all what God wants. The great principle found in this verse is connected to desiring what God wants for our lives. If our heart is tuned to pleasing God, His truth, His will, and His pleasure, then our desires will fall in line with His. As a result, we can be confident in asking for the good things that He has for us.

**PRAYER:** Dear God, I need Your grace to shape my heart. Many of the desires in my prayers frequently are only about what I want, not what You want. Draw me closer to Yourself. Help me see things through Your eyes.

# E

*__Encourage__ one another daily,*
*as long as it is called Today.*
Hebrews 3:13

As a young pastor, I remember hearing an older pastor in our Presbytery remark that he felt like quitting the ministry every Monday. It was discouraging for me to hear him say that. I was a bit young and eager and was sorry this pastor felt that way about his ministry. I later learned that he was a solo pastor in a church that was losing members and he felt all alone in his work. It revealed to me that at any stage of life, Christians need to be encouraged.

Courage is the quality of personal strength that enables us to face the challenges that come to us day by day. The believers who received this letter were facing many trials and difficulties. Some were considering renouncing their faith because denying it would make life easier. Each day, they needed the courage to stand for Christ in their daily walk.

Although it is true that God is there for us every step of the way, we get encouraged as we stand together in faith. The pastor I mentioned earlier needed someone to come alongside him, share his burdens, and speak God's Word to him in a way that would give him strength. We all need brothers and sisters who will encourage us. We need people who by their personal walk and faith and example inspire us. Our faith journey was never intended to be a solo trip.

**PRAYER:** Lord Jesus, You said that in this world we will have trouble. I know that to be true in my life, and I often get weary and discouraged. May I find the strength I need daily. Bring into my life loving and encouraging people who can support me, and I can help them.

# F

*"**For** you know the plans I have for you," declares
the LORD. "Plans to prosper you and not to
harm you, plans to give you hope and a future."*
Jeremiah 29:11

One year after I gave my life to Jesus, I had the opportunity to interview for the head football coaching job at Westminster High School, Westminster, Maryland. I had been an assistant coach for six years there and I thought as a head coach I would have the unique opportunity to influence young men and be a witness for Christ in the community. I truly thought it was God's will for my life to be the head football coach. The decision came down to either me or the other assistant coach.

About a week after my interview for the job, the principal of the school came to the athletic office and pulled me aside to tell me the decision. He told me that although he had never heard a better interview, the job was given to the other man because he had previous experience being a head coach.

Obviously disappointed by the news, I simply and sincerely said to my principal: "Pete, if God had wanted me to get the job, he would have given it to me." My principal gave no response to my answer, and that was that. I served the new coach the next season as his assistant to the best of my ability.

But God had a very different plan for me. At the end of the following football season, I felt called to become a pastor and seek the necessary training for such a calling. That summer we sold our home, and I moved my wife and three sons to St. Louis to study to become an ordained minister. This was indeed the plan that God had for me and my family.

**PRAYER:** Gracious Lord, You have plans for your children. May I believe in my heart You are working out your plan in my life.

# G

*__God__ is our refuge and strength,*
*an ever-present help in trouble.*
Psalm 46:1

The biblical word "refuge" is used repeatedly in the Old Testament to mean a "safe place." We live in a time when college campuses feel the need to provide this. These are designed to be a location where a student can go and not have to be confronted with an idea or opinion that may cause them stress. Colleges that seek to shelter their students with safe places are really doing a disservice to our young people.

At one time, being at college was considered a place to explore ideas and to have honest and open dialogue about what other people thought and believed. As my Christian family physician once said to me, "Sorry you are feeling stress, but life is stress."

Feeling stress is a natural response to conflict or trouble. Our pulse rate may go up, we may feel a bit panicky, and perhaps even have a feeling of impending doom. These are reactions to fear and are typical when we try to take responsibility to deal with our struggle in our own strength.

God wants to give us His strength when we face difficult circumstances. Psalm 46:1 reminds us that God not only cares about our worries, but He is ever-present to help us. If we call on Him, we know He hears us. And not only that He hears us, but that He will provide a place of safety. We can be confident He will supply the power to enable us to face whatever difficulty comes our way.

**PRAYER:** Gracious Lord, I do not know all that this day holds. There may be problems and situations today that may be troublesome. May I look to You for help to calm my spirit to deal with whatever stresses come my way.

# H

*__He__ himself is our peace.*
Ephesians 2:14

I have seen bumper stickers on cars that have the phrase, "Visualize World Peace." I want to ask those people, "What are you really trying to say with that slogan?"

Do they really believe they can have peace by merely imagining it in their minds? Such a view implies that the thoughts of a person are so powerful that they have the ability to impact the outcome of nations.

The real power in the universe is the Almighty God, the Creator of all things. Our greatest need is not world peace but peace with God. The gulf between the holy God of the Universe and sinful people is a vast chasm, greater than natural man can fathom. Yet in His infinite mercy, God has provided a way for breakers of His holy laws to have peace with Him.

That solution was given in the form of the incarnate Son of God, Jesus Christ. Jesus came to pay for our sins so the gulf between sinners and God could be breached. We can come to God in full fellowship if we come through faith through the atoning work of the resurrected Christ. He is the true source of peace.

**PRAYER:** Dear Jesus, thank You for the peace You have brought into my life. Through You, my sins are forgiven, and I can enter into fellowship with God the Father with boldness and confidence. May I never forget that it is because of You that I have this most wonderful privilege.

# I

*I tell you the truth, he who
believes has everlasting life.*
John 6:47

The night that I prayed to receive Jesus Christ into my life, the two men presenting the good news of God's grace asked me to do something. After I had prayed to accept Jesus as my Savior, they handed me a Bible and asked me to read John 6:47.

From the mouth of Jesus Himself, we have this great assurance of eternal life. Jesus had just previously shared that He was the "bread of life," the very source of spiritual life with God. He also stated in John 6:40, *"For my Father's will is for everyone who looks to the Son and believes in him shall have eternal life."*

The faith that gives this wonderful assurance is not "faith in faith" but faith in the person and work of Jesus Christ.

**PRAYER:** Dear Jesus, may I always believe that through You, and You alone, I have everlasting life. May I never forget to show You and tell You how thankful I am.

# J

*For the **joy** of the LORD is your strength.*
Nehemiah 8:10

There is a wonderful story behind this verse. Nehemiah spoke this to the people of God in the midst of one of the great revivals in the Old Testament. After the walls of Jerusalem had been rebuilt and the people felt safe, the next task was to rebuild the people's hearts. Ezra the priest brought out the Book of the Law and read it to the thousands that had gathered. Then, the Levites explained the meaning of what was read. As a result, the people became convicted of their sin and began to weep openly.

Nehemiah realizing that true repentance was occurring did not want this powerful movement of God to turn into great sorrow. To know God's character and know how to please Him as expressed in His Law was a wonderful privilege and a reason for rejoicing. So, He declared, *"Go and enjoy choice food and sweet drinks and send some to those who have nothing prepared. This day is sacred to the LORD. Do not grieve,* **for the joy of the LORD is your strength."**

~

**PRAYER:** Dear God, may I remember today that joy comes to me through a relationship with Your Son Jesus Christ, my risen and living Lord. May I rejoice that through Him my sins are forgiven, and I now have a new life and a new purpose.

# K

*And we **know** that in all things God works for the good of those who love him, who have been called according to his purpose.*
Romans 8:28

When I became a believer in Jesus Christ at age 28, my wife and I already had two sons with a third one only one month away. Our oldest son Michael was five and had already spent two years of his life with chronic lung problems. The doctors diagnosed his illness as infectious asthma and every time he got the common cold it would turn into pneumonia. From ages three to eight, he had pneumonia on twenty-seven occasions and was hospitalized twenty-three separate times.

During this trying season of our life, we came to cling to the promise of this wonderful verse. Although we could not understand why our little boy had to deal with this great affliction, knowing that God was in control and had a good plan for us and our son Michael gave us supernatural comfort.

By God's great mercy, our son's bouts of pneumonia stopped at age eight and never returned. And at this writing, Michael has three sons of his own, Max, Cole, and Graham, who, by God's grace, all enjoy good health.

～

**PRAYER:** Lord, help me to believe that in whatever trial I am experiencing right now, You care about me, and You are working in my life to bring good out of the situation. Give me the faith to believe this promise and the strength to trust in You.

# L

*__Love__ the Lord your God with all your
heart and with all your soul and with
all your mind and with all your strength.*
Mark 12:30

I have never met a person who said they have never sinned, but I have heard of such cases. I suppose if some people would believe this it is because they have never murdered someone or never robbed a bank. Because they have not committed some heinous sin, they have lived a life that in their eyes qualifies as sinless.

I have often thought, however, if I met someone who says they have never sinned, I would quote this verse and ask them if they have truly loved God with all their heart. Since this is the summary of all of God's laws, if they were truly honest, they could not say their love for God has been on this level.

There are many religions that make rule-keeping the standard for eternal life. But this verse, appropriately labeled the Great Commandment, emphasizes loving God with your entire being, not rule-keeping. Although we should strive to keep this commandment, the greatest of all standards, Romans 3:23 tells us, *"We all fall short."*

As beings with a natural sinful nature, we cannot keep the high standard of this commandment perfectly. That is why God had to send His perfect Son to be our Savior.

**PRAYER:** Gracious, Loving Father, help me to see the love You have for me through Jesus. Although I know I fail to keep this commandment every day, give me grace to enable me to love You more and more.

# M

*__My__ grace is sufficient for you, for my*
*power is made perfect in weakness.*
2 Corinthians 12:9

Some years ago, my wife and I spent three weeks traveling in Morocco visiting and encouraging missionaries. I have never felt more out of control in all my adult life. Not knowing the language and not knowing the travel routes made us completely dependent on our missionary hosts for food, lodging, and general survival.

Although it may sound a bit ironic, I also cannot remember a time when I felt the Lord's presence and protection more complete and more comforting. The saying that goes, "When God is all you have, you realize that God is all you need," rang true in our situation in Morocco.

The memory verse for today communicates this truth in a powerful way. Until we have to give up control and depend on God completely, we may not know just how powerful God can be.

**PRAYER:** Great and Powerful Lord, when I feel out of control, may I turn to You for Your all-sufficient grace and power. In the moments when I feel weak, may I look to You and believe You will give me whatever I need.

# N

*__Now__ that you know these things,*
*you will be blessed if you do them.*
John 13:17

In my career as a pastor for over forty years, this verse became more and more my own personal ministry philosophy. I have read many church purpose statements. Most talk about teaching God's Word and wanting people to be obedient to God's commands. But for me, I feel Jesus' words to His disciples in the Upper Room just hours before He would face the agony of the cross is so poignant. He didn't scold, become overly emotional, or give a dramatic speech. He said gently, follow my commandments and you will be blessed.

I do not deny that a pastor who loves his congregation should not hesitate to warn his flock of the dangers of sin. But Jesus offers a message of encouragement and hope with the gentleness that so typified His ministry. As I have frequently said to the people of Covenant of Grace, my job in preaching is largely to show them how to get blessed. And that route is clearly spelled out in this wonderful verse. Follow Jesus' words and life and you will find blessing.

**PRAYER:** Dear Jesus, thank You for reminding me that I need to apply what I learn. Forgive me for being content to just get facts and information and not seek to put what I know into the choices of my life.

# O

*To **obey** is better than sacrifice.*
1 Samuel 15:22

There is a powerful story behind this verse. It comes right before the prophet Samuel's statement to King Saul. Samuel tells him that because of his disobedience to God's direct command, he would be rejected as Israel's king. God had given Saul the command to destroy the Amalekites as His judgment against them. But out of self-serving motives, Saul chose to only partially obey. His excuse was that he was saving the best of the spoils of victory so he could make an offering to God. But God didn't want the offering. His instruction had been explicit. But Saul reasoned that he knew more than God.

We can all learn a valuable lesson here. Saul felt he could do whatever he wanted and if he was wrong, a few sacrifices would cover God's wrath. He was both arrogant and half-hearted in his devotion to the Lord. As we face temptations, we can come back to this verse and remember that God is pleased with our obedience.

**PRAYER:** Heavenly Father, forgive me for the times when I have disobeyed Your clear instruction in Scripture by presuming on Your grace and mercy. Help me to remember this verse so that I can resist the temptation to rationalize my disobedience.

# P

*The **plans** of the LORD stand firm forever,*
*the purposes of his heart through all generations.*
Psalm 33:11

In the summer after our first year at Covenant Theological Seminary in St. Louis, Missouri, my wife and I were surprised when we received a call from the senior pastor of our home church. He informed us that he and his wife were about to return to Maryland following a speaking engagement in Colorado. He asked if he could make a quick stop in St. Louis and visit us. Of course, we were delighted.

Upon arriving at our home, he told us that his main reason for visiting was to see if we would be interested in returning to Maryland, and for me to serve as his intern pastor. The job also included the possibility of starting a mission church in the nearby town of Reisterstown after I had finished my second year at Covenant Seminary. A program had been developed so I could complete the final year of my MDiv degree at Westminster Theological Seminary in Philadelphia.

I had already been contacted by a church in Dallas to be an intern pastor there. But the idea of returning to where we grew up and starting a church was beyond any expectations we had had.

One of the great assurances to our faith is the knowledge that God goes before us, and His good purposes do not change. Things constantly change around us all the time. But to know that God's plan is perfect and unchangeable, should be a great source of comfort to us.

**PRAYER:** Almighty God, You are the Sovereign Lord. Nothing is going to happen to me today that will come as a surprise to You. I can live with confidence knowing that whatever comes my way is under Your control.

# Q

*Everyone should be **quick** to listen,
slow to speak, and slow to become angry.*
James 1:19

My dad was in so many ways a wonderful example to me. He never cursed, smoked or drank alcohol. He was a man of great integrity and never failed to take us to church every Sunday.

Looking back from a biblical perspective, however, one problem my dad did have was anger. He was a strict disciplinarian as a father and controlled us with angry looks and an angry tone in his voice. While I never doubted his love for me, as a child I feared his outbursts of anger.

The Bible warns of the sins of the father being passed on for generations (Exodus 34:7). I freely admit I have struggled with anger. If the Minirth-Meier Clinic's definition is accurate, "depression is anger turned inward," I know I have personally dealt with this at times.

The book of James has been called the wisdom book of the

New Testament. While it has no historical narrative section, it is filled with short, profound bits of wisdom that speak to living the Christian life in wise and practical ways.

Our "Q" verse is a very clear example. How many times in our life have we quickly blurted out something in anger? When I was a child, my mother would often quote to me, "Sticks and stones may break my bones, but words will never hurt me," but the Bible says this is not true. Angry words can cause deep hurt. Our memory verse for today is advice from God on how to prevent this.

**PRAYER:** Father, help me to memorize this verse and apply it to my everyday life. May my words reflect the grace and compassion of Jesus, my true example.

# R

*__Rejoice__ in the Lord always. I will say it again: Rejoice! Let your gentleness be evident to all. The Lord is near.*
Philippians 4:4–5

In the nineteenth year of my ministry at Covenant of Grace, I experienced serious depression. Besides feeling tired all the time and having a general attitude of discouragement, I had lost any real enthusiasm for my future ministry. I intentionally avoided stressful situations and chose not to deal with people that were hurting.

After having my family doctor confirm that I was clinically depressed, I shared my struggle with my Session of Elders and asked for help. They gave me a ten-week leave of absence and encouraged me to get some professional counseling. The medication my doctor prescribed for the physiological component of my depression began to take effect in about two weeks.

After that, I was able to get up early, read my Bible, and enjoy extended times of prayer with the Lord. The counselor I was seeing also showed me some significant things about myself that I needed to understand and change. Reading the Bible, especially Paul's letter to the Philippians ministered to my soul. His writing about having joy and contentment despite being in prison were words that God used to help lift me out of my depression and discouragement.

I came back to my duties as a pastor to a very difficult church-wide problem that had escalated while I was away. But God had healed me of my clinical depression, and I was now able to deal with that situation effectively and go on to serve the church for an additional twenty years without a reoccurrence.

**PRAYER:** Jesus, may I remember that, whenever I get discouraged, You are my Living Lord and near to help. Life is full of stress and disappointments. But You have a plan to redeem the earth and knowing that, I can rejoice again and again. May I remember how You have helped me in the past so I can be confident that You will provide for me in the future.

# S

*Seek first his kingdom and his righteousness,
and all these things will be given to you as well.*
Matthew 6:33

Coming to faith in the seventies, I had the advantage of an era of Christian music that was saturated with what was called "Scripture Songs." Song after song was just pure scripture, most often lifted from the King James version of the Bible. I loved a particular song we regularly sang for about two decades: "Seek ye first the kingdom of God and his righteousness. And all these things shall be added unto you. Hallelu, Hallelujah."

Singing scripture is one of the best ways to memorize scripture. Somehow a good melody with a consistent beat allows the brain to permanently record a verse in our head. The great challenge of course is to put the meaning of the song into practice in our lives. I hope you know this song and can sing it and know the great challenge and blessing it promises.

**PRAYER:** Heavenly Father, I confess I am too often self-absorbed with my own concerns. Help me to make seeking what pleases You to be the priority of my life. Show me what You want me to do this day.

T

*__Therefore__ go and make disciples of all nations, baptizing them in the name of the Father and of the Son and of the Holy Spirit, and teaching them to obey everything I have commanded you.*
Matthew 28:19–20

Our middle son, Bradley, had a real burden for his friends to come to know Jesus as their Savior. During his junior and senior years in high school, he would bring three or four of his buddies to church and then to our home for lunch after worship. I believe that investment helped two of them become church members, one was baptized, and one went to seminary after college and was ordained and led campus ministry on several large universities.

Jesus came to give us forgiveness and the assurance of eternal life, but also a purpose. Before Jesus ascended to heaven, He gave His disciples a final word of instruction popularly known as the "Great Commission." One purpose in a Christian's life is to make disciples. The word "go" in verse 19 in the original language is not a command; it is a participle. A more literal translation of the beginning of this verse would be, "As you are going."

"Make disciples" is the actual command. Developing committed followers of Jesus Christ is the real objective of the Great Commission, whether in foreign lands or in your own backyard.

~

**PRAYER:** Dear Jesus, help me to see the people around me that I can influence. Give me the boldness to share my faith with others and be faithful to the Great Commission.

# U

*__Unless__ the LORD builds the house,*
*its builders labor in vain.*
Psalm 127:1

When I became a committed follower of Jesus Christ at age 28, I had two sons, Michael (5), Bradley (4), and a third son, Mark, only a month away from being born. Coming to know my sins were forgiven and that I was an eternal child of God gave me a spiritual high that lasted for weeks.

But soon after coming to faith, I wondered: "What about my kids?" I had this great joy and excitement because I was eternally secure in Jesus, but I had this incredibly deep desire for my sons to have that same faith.

Fortunately, my wife and I had become connected to a wonderful gospel-centered church, and a visit from the pastor explained that God had special promises to our children as well. Before Mark, our youngest son, was baptized, we received instruction from our pastor regarding God's covenant promise to the children of believers.

When our two older boys had been baptized, I had no comprehension of the nature of God's covenant promise to our children. But now, with an understanding of Genesis 17:7 and Acts 2:38, I had great joy knowing that my Lord also loved my children and promised to be in their lives.

**PRAYER:** Gracious Father, thank You for the precious promises You make to parents who have put their trust in Jesus. I pray that You would build families would seek to put You first.

# V

*This is the **verdict**: Light
has come into the world.*
John 3:19

One of my favorite stories in the Bible is found in John's gospel in Chapter 9. It is a detailed account of how Jesus heals a blind man, a story filled with exciting details.

First, Jesus puts a mud potion on the man's eyes and tells him to go to a special place and wash. Meanwhile, Jesus has slipped away.

After the man washes, he can see. He is then interrogated about this miracle by the religious officials. All he knows is the man's name was Jesus. The Pharisees do everything they can to discredit this event. Even the parents are quizzed, but they fear repercussions if they give Jesus the credit.

But the former blind man gets bolder and bolder as the Pharisees call Jesus a sinner because the healing was done on the

Sabbath. It is not until the man is thrown out of the synagogue for his testimony of his faith in Jesus that he gets to meet Jesus.

When Jesus asks him if he believes in Him as the "Son of Man," the man born blind responds: *"'Lord I believe,' and he worshipped him."* (John 9:38) Jesus then says: *"For judgment I have come into the world so that the blind will see and those who can see will become blind"* (John 9:39).

There can be no neutrality with Jesus. After He gives the great offer of salvation in Him, (John 3:16), Jesus states that His coming into the world gives men a clear choice. They can either stay in the dark, i.e., the state of mind of loving evil, or they can come to Him and experience the light.

**PRAYER:** Dear Jesus, You are the light of the world. You came so I could see my sin and know the cleansing that comes from Your forgiveness. Help me to testify to the world who You are and walk in Your light day by day.

# W

*__Work__ out your salvation with fear and trembling
for it is God who works in you to will and to
act according to his good purpose.*
Philippians 2:12–13

I remember a conversation I once had with a student while I was still teaching at Westminster High School. She had heard I had become a believer in Jesus and wanted to talk to me after class about my faith. Unfortunately, she really wanted to talk to me so she could correct a doctrinal error she thought I had.

She steered the conversation into her strong conviction that the doctrine of "eternal security" was wrong. To her, it was clear that faith alone in Jesus was not enough. With with a touch of arrogance, she quoted the first half of today's memory verse, *"Work out your salvation with fear and trembling."* To her, that was proof enough that "good works" was the basis for salvation.

She was surprised when I quoted the rest of the verse to counter her argument. I reminded her that it speaks of God's sovereign work as the basis for our salvation, and I quoted Ephesians 2:8–9 to her, which emphasizes that faith, not works is the basis for eternal life.

She turned and went away without giving a rebuttal.

Although we are commanded to do good works as children of God, we must never forget that we are totally dependent on God for the results. While we are to be working, we need to remember that God too, is working. (John 5:17) He is continually involving Himself in our lives to empower us and to enable us to do the good things that He has planned for us to do. The fear and trembling mentioned is not some slavish fear. It is the feeling of deep respect that someone so great as God would invest Himself personally in us.

**PRAYER:** Father, too often I live my life on my own strength. I confess I sometimes live as if I am the one who controls my destiny. Please remind me that You are intimately involved in my life, and that any progress I make in my spiritual journey is because You are working in me.

# X

*Righteousness **e(x)alts** a nation,*
*but sin is a disgrace to any people.*
Proverbs 14:34

The famous French statesman, historian, and social philosopher Alex de Tocqueville toured America in 1831 and wrote a two-part work in 1835 entitled, *Democracy in America*. It was described as the most comprehensive and penetrating analysis of the relationship between character and society in America that has ever been written (William J. Fedderer's "America's God and Country," p. 204).

In his book, de Toqueville stated:

I do not know whether all Americans have a sincere faith in their religion—for who can search the human heart? But I am certain that they hold to be indispensable to the maintenance of republican institutions. This opinion is not peculiar to a class of citizens or a party but belongs to the whole nation and to every rank of society.

Proverbs 14:34 is a grave warning for us in America today. Anyone who understands our religious heritage and the teachings of the Bible knows that the majority of our country's leaders are taking us farther and farther away from the biblical values that were fundamental to the foundation of our nation.

May memorizing this verse remind us to fervently pray for God's mercy and ask Him to send the spirit of revival into our hearts. May the people of this land repent of their sins and return to the principles in the Bible that made this country great.

**PRAYER:** Heavenly Father, in the USA, we have been given so many blessings from Your hand. Forgive our ungrateful independence and arrogant self-reliance. I pray for Your mercy to reign down and cause us as a nation to repent of our sin and seek Your righteous ways. As I pray for my country, I pray You would begin with me.

# Y

*__You__ will seek me and find me when
you seek me with all your heart.*
Jeremiah 29:13

My wife and I had our first grandchild, Blake, at age 49. Since then, God has given us four more grandsons, Max, Carter, Cole, and Graham, three granddaughters, Anna, Arabella, and Mae, and a great-granddaughter, Jane. One of the great joys of having grandchildren is that you can relive some of the precious, fun experiences you had when your own children were small.

One of the favorite games we had with our two youngest granddaughters, Arabella and Mae, was playing Hide-and-Seek in our house. It was a joy to see them love the idea of hiding, even in a place where they were barely hiding at all. Being found was what they really loved, and they often let out a squeal of delight. They also got excited when they found me hidden behind a curtain or a door. Finding someone they loved and someone who loved them gave them joy.

I believe that God loves to be found as well. When you love someone, you naturally want to be with them. God desires our love, therefore, He wants us to seek Him. David reminds us of this when he says *"My heart says of you, Seek his face! Your face LORD I will seek."* (Psalm 27:8).

What is so significant about this memory verse is that God indeed promises to be found. Our efforts in seeking Him will not go unrewarded. If we seek God with our whole heart, He will be found.

**PRAYER:** Living Lord, there are times when You have seemed far away. But I know that it is my sin causing the distance, not Your lack of love and care. May I show my love for You by seeking You in prayer, in worship, and in reading Your Word.

# Z

*It is not good to have*
*__zeal__ without knowledge.*
Proverbs 19:2

When I was called as organizing pastor of a mission church, I found that many people were drawn to us because they had been hurt in their previous church experience and were looking for a place to heal. A famous pastor once said that "the church is a hospital where people come to be healed."

We wanted our church to be a fellowship where people could find grace and healing. But sometimes the church can be a place where people can be emotionally hurt by those who express zeal without knowledge. Sadly, my wife had such an experience.

When our oldest son Michael was five and having serious lung problems, he spent five days at Johns Hopkins Hospital receiving tests. One complicated lung exam required general anesthesia. While he was still in the recovery room, an assistant pastor we had never met burst into the recovery room uninvited and said to my wife, "Are you willing to give your son to the Lord today?"

His words were full of zeal, but his ignorance of the situation and his assumption that she should demonstrate faith in God by accepting our son's possible death was extremely hurtful. We later came to appreciate his zeal for evangelism. But when he acted with such ignorance of our situation, we lacked confidence in his judgment in future circumstances.

This wisdom from Proverbs contains both a caution and a teaching point. If we lack knowledge of a person's situation, we are wise to withhold advice. Even then, a serious conversation with a person we do not know should be done with "gentleness and respect," as Peter instructs in 1 Peter 3:15.

**PRAYER:** Lord, may my zeal for You and Your Word be combined with knowledge as well as compassion and love that comes from knowing Jesus.

# PART TWO
# FAITH

# FAITH

In Scripture, faith generally refers to a living, personal trust in Jesus.

While it is important to see intimate fellowship with God as its primary aspect, faith also involves recognizing that certain things are true and we should give mental assent to them. Believing in Christ means assenting to the truth about Christ as well as coming to know Him.

True faith takes its character and quality from its object and not from itself. Faith gets a man out of himself and into Christ.

—Excerpts from Sinclair B. Ferguson, *The Christian Life*, p. 59–60

## LIST OF FAITH VERSES

"**Ask** and it will be given to you; seek and you will find; knock and the door will be opened to you."
Matthew 7:7

"**But** those who hope in the LORD will renew their strength. They will soar on wings like eagles; they will run and not grow weary, they will walk and not be faint."
Isaiah 40.31

"**Consider** it pure joy, my brothers, when you face trials of many kinds because you know that the testing of your faith develops perseverance."
James 1:2

"**Do** not fear, for I have redeemed you; I have called you by name; you are Mine!"
Isaiah 43:1 NASB

"I lift up my **eyes** to the hills. Where does my help come from? My help comes from the LORD, the Maker of heaven and earth."
Psalm 121:1

"**Faith** comes from hearing the message, and the message is heard through the word of Christ."
Romans 10:1

"**God** demonstrates his own love in this: While we were still sinners, Christ died for us."
Romans 5:8

"In **him** and through faith in him we may approach God with freedom and confidence."
Ephesians 3:12

"**I** can do all things through Christ who strengthens me."
Philippians 4:13 NKJV

"**Join** me in my struggle by praying to God for me."
Romans 15:30

"**Know** that the LORD, he is God: It is he who has made us and not we ourselves."
Psalm 100:3 NKJV

"**Live** by faith, not by sight."
2 Corinthians 5:7

"**My** soul finds rest in God alone; my salvation comes from him."
Psalm 62:1

"**Now** faith is the assurance of things hoped for, the conviction of things not seen."
Hebrews 11:1 NASB

"The **only** thing that counts is faith expressing itself through love."
Galatians 5:6

"**Pray** continually."
1 Thessalonians 5:17

"You **quarrel** and fight. You do not have, because you do not ask God."
James 4:2

"The **righteous** will live by faith."
Romans 1:17

"David found **strength** in the LORD his God."
1 Samuel 30:6

**"Trust** in the LORD with all your heart and lean not on your own understanding; in all your ways acknowledge him, and he will make your paths straight."
Proverbs 3:5-6

"I do believe. Help me overcome my **unbelief**!"
Mark 9:24

"This is the **victory** that has overcome the world, even our faith."
1 John 5:4

**"Without** faith it is impossible to please God, for anyone who comes to him must believe he exists and that he rewards those who earnestly seek him."
Hebrews 11:6

"**E(x)cel** in everything, in faith, in speech, in knowledge, in complete earnestness and in your love."
2 Corinthians 8:7

'**Yea,** though I walk through the valley of the shadow of death, I will fear no evil: for You are with me."
Psalm 23:4 NKJV

"The **zeal** of the LORD Almighty will accomplish this."
Isaiah 37:32

# A

*__Ask__ and it will be given to you; seek and you will find; knock and the door will be opened to you.*
Matthew 7:7

It may be a cliché, but why is it so difficult for men to ask their wives for directions when driving? This may be more true for the Baby Boomer generation, the age group that began driving before GPS became a routine tool for navigation. Regardless of the generational issue, a lack of humility and a cultural expectation of masculine pride may also be involved here.

Matthew 7:7 is one of the most instructive passages on prayer in the Bible. Praying to a God we cannot physically see or hear audibly takes faith. What we need to do is humble ourselves and acknowledge our need for the Lord.

Fortunately, in this passage of Scripture, Jesus shows us how to persevere in prayer through a progression of growing intensity. Sometimes prayer is just simply asking. Other times, our praying may take the form of actively pursuing God. For that, we need to seek. And at other times, we may need to be even more forceful in our requests.

This would be more like knocking. But notice what Jesus says: the result of each type of effort will be that God will hear and answer.

**PRAYER:** Lord Jesus, help me to actively pursue You in prayer. You have promised to hear and answer. But You also remind me that You want to be sought after. May I remember that my seeking You and making an effort to have my requests be heard is part of Your plan for building my faith.

# B

*__But__ those who hope upon the LORD will renew their strength. They will soar on wings like eagles; they will run and not grow weary; they will walk and not be faint.*
Isaiah 40:31

Have you ever seen a bald eagle in flight? Eagles primarily eat fish, so you will only see them near rivers, lakes, or large bodies of water.

As a whitewater kayak enthusiast, over the years, I have had numerous opportunities to see bald eagles in the wild which is always amazing. They are so big, and it's incredible that they can fly at all, much less do so with a large fish tucked away in their talons.

What makes our memory verse so vivid is that if you watch an eagle in flight, they rarely flap their wings. They use rising air currents to soar through the air until they reach their nest.

Isaiah says that hope is like that. Hope can simply be defined as future faith. And by believing in God's promises for the future, we can experience God's power to lift us with the strength that He supplies.

Our faith is like the wings of the eagle. It gives us the ability to take hold of the power of God like the wind that empowers that noble bird. And if we will trust God for His strength, we won't become weak and faint, but we will soar.

**PRAYER:** Gracious God, You are my source of hope. When I begin to tire in my walk of faith, help me remember that You promise to lift me up. Keep me encouraged knowing that You are not only walking beside me but that You are able to help me soar whenever I call on You.

# C

*__Consider__ it pure joy, my brothers, when you*
*face trials of many kinds, because you know*
*that the testing of your faith develops perseverance.*
James 1:2

I had the privilege of growing up in the town where the Baltimore Colts had their preseason training camp. I would often go to watch my favorite football player, Raymond Berry. After eleven seasons with the Colts, he set NFL records for most receptions, most yardage, and most touchdowns by a wide receiver.

A lot of people do not know the many obstacles he had to overcome to even make the team. He was not particularly successful in college, he was not very fast, one of his legs was shorter than the other, he was of a slight build, and he was a twentieth-round draft choice.

I remember watching him practice with quarterback Johnny Unitas. Berry worked at catching passes from difficult angles for an extra thirty minutes or more after all the other players had finished practicing. As a college football player myself, I sought to emulate his example of persevering through adversity.

Combining trials with joy seems like a contradiction. But to James, for faith to be real, it has to be tested. When we face difficulties and we continue to believe in the goodness and faithfulness of God, we show that our faith is genuine. When we persevere through trials, it shows that we are becoming more like our Savior, and knowing this should give us joy whatever the circumstance.

**PRAYER:** Lord, this is hard teaching. My first response to trials is often to complain and doubt Your goodness. Help me remember that Your Son constantly underwent trials and persevered. May my growing in faith despite trials give me joy.

# D

*__Do__ not fear, for I have redeemed you;*
*I have called you by name; you are Mine!*
Isaiah 43:1 NASB

Several years ago, I developed a serious fear of driving over large bodies of water. I believe that started after I read about a fatal accident when a car plunged over the Chesapeake Bay Bridge. In the past, I had enjoyed glancing at the sailboats off in the distance. But now, I found myself frozen in fear merely approaching the bridge.

I believed this fear was irrational. Deep down I knew that I was in God's hands regardless of the circumstance. My fear made me feel embarrassed and ashamed.

So what did I do?

I took out my Bible concordance and began researching every reference containing the word "fear." After a brief study, I was drawn to Isaiah 43:1. Not only did it command me not to be afraid, but it also reminded me that I was God's child and in His care. I belonged to Him and having that assurance was what I needed to overcome my fear.

The next time I drove across the Chesapeake Bay Bridge, I continually recited this verse. All the fear did not dissipate initially.

But each time I faced this challenge and recited this verse, my fears lessened. Now, years later, I'm fine driving over bridges, due very much in part to my memorizing and reciting this scripture verse. God's Word can truly impact your life.

**PRAYER:** Father, thank You for your Word and its power. Knowing Your Word by heart is like having You speak to me personally. May I strive to memorize these verses so I can be prepared in an instant to hear You speak words of assurance.

# E

*I lift up my __eyes__ unto the hills—where
does my help come from? My help comes from
the LORD, the Maker of heaven and earth.*
Psalm 121:1

I have stood at many hospital bedsides over the last four decades, and there is no Scripture that has consistently brought more comfort to those who are suffering than this verse. The psalmist writes as if he is peering into the future, anticipating his life full of difficulties and challenges. And to finish this journey, he needs help. He knows the very best person to assist him is the Maker of the Universe, whom he has called on time after time.

This verse describes what true faith is like. It looks up and trusts in the One who is above us and beyond us. His promises give us hope and encouragement, particularly in difficult times with words He alone has the power to deliver. The psalm ends with this wonderful promise: *"The Lord will keep you from all harm—he will watch over your life; the Lord will watch over your coming and going, both now and forevermore"* (Psalm 121:7–8).

**PRAYER:** Lord, I am indeed on a journey. Help me to "look up" when trouble surrounds me. Give me the faith to believe You are always with me and that I can trust You for strength along the way.

# F

*__Faith__ comes from hearing the message, and the
message is heard through the word of Christ.*
Romans 10:17

Although I did not come to personal faith in Jesus Christ until I was 28, I am so thankful that my parents took me to Sunday School and church for the first 17 years of my life. When I began to study the Bible in earnest after putting my faith in Jesus, so much of what I had been taught as a child came back to me and then made sense.

Romans 10:17 explains that we cannot have a correct understanding of the teachings of the Bible without a right knowledge of Jesus Christ. We must always remember that our Christian faith is faith in Him, not faith in faith. Our ability to understand the Bible correctly comes through having new life in the One who died for us and rose again and is the reason for our salvation.

**PRAYER:** Lord Jesus, there are so many benefits to faith. Through faith I have confidence. I have contentment. I have a sure hope for the future. May I never forget that these benefits come to me because of your life, death, and resurrection.

# G

*__God__ demonstrates his own love for us in this:*
*while we were still sinners, Christ died for us.*
Romans 5:8

When I was 17, I attended a week-long Fellowship of Christian Athletes Camp in upstate New York. The theme of the camp was "Inspiration and Perspiration." We enjoyed intense sports competition, but also spent time studying the Bible in our "huddle groups." In the evening, we would have a time of singing hymns and a talk from a well-known college or professional athlete or coach, who would speak about the blessings of following Jesus.

On the final day after the evening talk, we were encouraged to go off alone, and if we had never done so, invite Jesus Christ into our lives to be our Lord and Savior. I remember vividly stopping under a tall tree and simply telling God, "I can't do it." I knew if I asked Jesus to come into my life, I would have to change some things, and I wasn't willing to do that.

Ten years later in my family room, in front of my believing

wife and two men who shared the message of salvation with me, I surrendered my life to Christ. I asked God to forgive my sins, and I asked Jesus to come into my life and be my Lord and Savior.

Even when I was coming under the conviction that Jesus was indeed my personal Savior, I remembered how ten years earlier I had rejected Jesus' offer and chose to push Him away. That night I understood deep in my heart the meaning of today's memory verse. Even in my rebellion and despite my refusing His offer in the past, Jesus still had loved me and had gone to the cross for me.

**PRAYER:** Father, may I never take Your love for granted or think that somehow through my effort or my own goodness I discovered You. Help me live my life as a continuous Thank You for loving me through the gift of Your Son Jesus Christ.

# H

*In __him__ and through faith in him we may*
*approach God with freedom and confidence.*
Ephesians 3:12

There are many mysterious things about the Christian life. I like to think of myself as an honest pursuer of truth. Frankly, I try to come up with a reasonable explanation for the things that happen.

But one of the wonderful things about knowing God is that because He is so great, there will be events and circumstances that we could never understand with our limited intelligence. One of the blessings of faith is being content in knowing that some things will remain a mystery. But that is okay. God has a plan and is working out that plan.

This verse also speaks to a profound question. With all the people in the world, how could God possibly hear every single voice of those who go to Him in prayer? But here we are told we can be confident that we have free access to God at any moment.

We never have to worry that He is too busy or unable to hear our prayers.

~

**PRAYER:** This verse reminds me that You are my Father who cares and listens to my prayers. But it also tells me of the incredible privilege I have as Your child, that I always have access to you through faith in Your Son Jesus Christ.

# I

*I can do all things through*
*Christ who strengthens me.*
Philippians 4:13 NKJV

I have a personal connection to this verse because if you asked my wife, Shelley, for her favorite verse in the Bible she would say it's Philippians 4:13.

She suffered a severe knee injury from a sledding accident when she was 17. Since then, she has had nine knee operations and several severe complications following some of those surgeries. She also has survived breast cancer, has had back surgery, and deals with a rare immune disorder that affects all her joints. But she never complains and has accomplished so many things in her life and continues at a pace that is truly remarkable.

When I asked her why Philippians 4:13 meant so much to her, the word she used was "courage." Her faith in the strength she receives from her relationship with Christ gives her courage to face life's constant challenges despite the pain she deals with every day.

Yet beginning every morning with her daily devotional time with Jesus, she lives life with great energy, enthusiasm, and purpose because she trusts Jesus to give her strength.

**PRAYER:** May I believe that through faith in You, I can do all things that You desire me to do. Give me the courage to do the right thing and please You with my choices. Help me to live with purpose and vitality knowing that through faith in You, I can receive strength for every challenge.

# J

*__Join__ me in my struggle by*
*praying to God for me.*
Romans 15:30

Several years ago, my friend Rod Hairston, who at the time was the chaplain of the Baltimore Ravens, asked me to speak at one of their pre-game chapel services. I was deeply honored to be able to share in front of so many prestigious professional athletes.

I asked Chaplain Hairston if I could talk about the value of memorizing Scripture, and he gave me an enthusiastic "Yes!" I must admit, I was initially a bit star-struck in front of the team. But as I proceeded to talk about the tremendous value of Scripture memory and gave specific examples from my list of Encouragement verses, I saw a genuine interest.

Romans 15:30 seemed to resonate with their commitment to each other as teammates. Football is truly a team sport. The Apostle Paul is saying, "When you pray to God on a person's behalf, you enter into a personal relationship with them. If I am suffering, and you pray for me, you somehow share in that suffering with me. This gives us a bond that is very special."

After my talk on Scripture memory, I handed out a sheet of paper to all the players containing the Encouragement verses, and each of the players and coaches shook my hand and thanked me.

**PRAYER:** Father, I appreciate the great privilege of prayer. Thank You for allowing my prayers to draw me close to You. In turn, help me experience an increased closeness to those I pray with and pray for.

# K

*__Know__ that the L*ORD*, he is God. It is*
*he who has made us, and not we ourselves.*
Psalm 100:3 NKJV

I was blessed with a godly mother-in-law, Doris Armacost, who was also very talented musically. When we began as a mission church in Reisterstown, she joined our core group, and even at 73, she played the electric organ for our worship services for the next ten years.

At 91, she had a slight stroke that permanently affected her balance, and she needed to enter an assisted living facility. Doris became a true evangelist there, never tiring of inviting the other residents to weekly Bible study and to the Sunday afternoon chapel services. Her favorite pastime was memorizing the Scriptures that the chaplain would challenge them to learn every week.

As she neared her 103rd birthday, unable to swallow, and near her time to be with the Lord, as her pastor for nearly 30 years, I went to visit her. I had been told by her Stephen Minister that her favorite passage of Scripture was Psalm 123. After reading it to her, she commented, "Herb, that does not sound familiar." (Psalm 123 is not well known.)

Very soon after reading it, her eldest daughter came into her room, and I explained how Psalm 123 hadn't seemed right to Doris. After a brief chuckle, her daughter Dinah explained that she had told the Stephen Minister that Psalm 100 and Psalm 23 were her mother's favorites—not Psalm 123. I then gladly read those to her.

Two days later, she went to be in the presence of the Lord who had made her, sustained her, and called her home.

**PRAYER:** Father, I know I have at times seemingly given myself the credit for my successes. How short-sighted I am in forgetting that You made me. Any achievements I have accomplished are only because You created me with gifts and talents. Help me to be quick to give You credit in my heart and praise in public for whatever successes I accomplish.

# L

*__Live__ by faith, not by sight.*
2 Corinthians 5:7

I met Laura Story at a Christian music leadership conference in Spartanburg, South Carolina, before she became a well-known Christian singer, songwriter, and author. At the time, she was merely introduced as the worship leader at the Perimeter Church in Atlanta when my wife and I attended her small group talk.

When it came time for her to address the 1,500 attendees at the conference, she was introduced as the composer of the popular worship song, "Indescribable." Everyone perked up to hear her inspiring words.

She had married her high school sweetheart right after college. But in the second year of their marriage, her husband, Martin Elvington, was diagnosed with a major brain tumor. Complications after his surgery left him permanently disabled in his vision and memory. Their plans were forever altered.

Still married since 2005, they now have four children, and

Laura has gone on to win many music awards. Her original song "Blessings" won a Grammy Award, and her follow-up book with the subtitle *What If Blessings Come Through Raindrops* has been a great encouragement, especially to people who have had life-altering circumstances. In *So Long Normal: Living and Loving the Free Fall of Faith*, she writes that she hears God saying, "Find that security in me. Find that stability and value in me." That is what living by faith and not by sight is all about.

**PRAYER:** Lord, I know there are no guarantees in this life other than Your unfailing love and faithfulness. Help me to live trusting in Your plan, knowing my only real security is in You.

# M

*__My__ soul finds rest in God alone;*
*my salvation comes from him.*
Psalm 62:1

Our third son, Mark, was born just one month after I came to know the Lord. My wife and I gave him the middle name Christian in part because it reminded us of two very special days in our lives —his birth and my rebirth. I can easily remember how long I have been trusting in Jesus by remembering the age of my youngest son.

When Mark was still little, I heard John Michael Talbot sing a paraphrased version of Psalm 62:1–2 entitled, *Psalm 62 (Only in God).* The tune is very close to the melodic phrasing of a lullaby.

For many years, I would sing that rendition of Psalm 62 when I put Mark to bed. I don't remember when that routine stopped, but it is a treasured memory for me, and I hope for him.

The psalm's message is beautiful and clear. Rest for your soul comes from God alone. You cannot find that ultimate rest anywhere else but in the arms of our Lord.

Listen to the song on YouTube.

**PRAYER:** Heavenly Father, may I find more and more that the first thing I really need to do is to be quiet before You, rest in You, and know that You are God.

# N

*__Now__ faith is the assurance of things hoped
for, the conviction of things not seen.*
Hebrews 11:1 NASB

In the fall of 1978, my wife and I felt a strong call from God that I should go to seminary and pursue pastoral ministry, which would mean facing many challenges to us and our faith. It meant quitting my job, selling our home, and moving away from our family.

In addition, our oldest son had a chronic lung problem and had been hospitalized 23 times within the previous 5 years. We lived next door to my wife's parents. They were invaluable in helping take care of our two younger sons when our oldest had to stay in the hospital an average of seven days each time before he was well enough to come home. On top of that, my wife had a knee problem that required surgery.

On December 1, 1978, my wife and I made the decision that God would provide all that we needed, and we would go to St. Louis and study for the ministry even though there were still several unresolved issues. We were convicted God wanted us to go, and we should trust Him for all we needed.

That December, my wife had a knee revision operation that was unsuccessful and the surgeon said she might always need a cane to walk. But we continued to step out in faith.

In time, God healed our oldest son's lung problem, our house was sold without a realtor, and the inheritance my mother willed us provided for our three-and-one-half years in seminary.

Faith is being assured that God is working and will enable you to do His will even if the details are unclear.

**PRAYER:** Lord, give me the faith to follow wherever You lead. May I have the conviction that You will be faithful to provide whatever my needs might be.

# O

*The **only** thing that counts is
faith expressing itself through love.*
Galatians 5:6

When we were starting Covenant of Grace Church, we were looking for a slogan and byline that could summarize who we wanted to be as a church. We wanted it to be short, to the point, and memorable. We chose Galatians 5:6 for that purpose.

We wanted to be a church that believed that faith in Jesus as Savior and Lord was essential, and that that faith was based on the truth of God's Word.

But we also were aware that sometimes people can share their faith in a way that is not loving or gracious. Paul's statement to the churches in Galatia says so clearly that our faith must be expressed in a loving way.

Although Covenant of Grace Church no longer uses this verse as its slogan, the goal of living out our faith in Jesus Christ in love is what we know really counts. And that belief has never changed.

**PRAYER:** Heavenly Father, may I never forget that the faith that brought me to Christ came from Your heart of love. May my faith cause me to grow deeper in love with You and with others.

# P

*__Pray__ continually.*
1 Thessalonians 5:17

My wife, Shelley, made a sincere profession of faith when she was 17. I was a regular church attender when we got married while still in college, but I was not a follower of Christ.

In her early twenties, my wife recommitted her life to Jesus, and she had a burning desire for me to know Jesus as my Savior as well. So at 23, she would call her sister who lived five hours away, and they prayed for me. They kept up this routine of praying for my salvation for five years.

On September 9, 1976, their prayers were answered. I bowed my head, opened my heart, and asked Jesus to forgive my sins and be my Savior and Lord.

My life is a living example that God may not give us the answer to our prayers immediately, but He will answer. There may be times when we must pray continually and for long periods of time. My wife prayed for five years before receiving her answer.

So when God does not respond as fast as we would like, remember this verse and testimonies like mine to strengthen your faith and persevere in prayer.

**PRAYER:** Father, You tell us to pray continually. That can be hard because we impatiently expect quick results. Help me develop a life of continuous prayer for what I need and not necessarily for what I want. But above all, may I strive to please you.

# Q

*You **quarrel** and fight. You do not*
*have, because you do not ask God.*
James 4:2

James prefaces this verse with the question, *"What causes fights and quarrels among you?"* Then he answers, saying, *"Don't they come from your desires that battle within you?"*

Self-centeredness is at the core of many of our conflicts. I wonder how many marriage quarrels could be avoided by remembering this verse and asking for God's perspective on an issue before stating our own view as paramount.

One of the powerful things about prayer is that sincere prayer has as its motive not only our felt need but a desire to please God as well. Perhaps it would behoove Christian couples to remember this verse and be quick to pray for God's leading before a quarrel even begins.

**PRAYER:** Father, I confess that I am prone to be self-centered and believe that I am always right. When I sense a quarrel is beginning to develop, may I be quick to ask for Your guidance so my words would express Your will and Your love in what I say and do.

# R

*The **righteous** will live by faith.*
Romans 1:17

Martin Luther's understanding of this verse changed his life—and history. He had struggled with the sense of his inability to merit forgiveness for his sin. He would agonize over his sin and incessantly have no hope of relief.

However, by studying this verse, Luther came to understand that righteousness can only come to us as a gift. It cannot be earned or deserved.

Through Jesus Christ's perfect life and substitutionary death on the cross, Christ transfers His righteousness to anyone who receives Him by faith. That understanding is the very essence of the Gospel.

That we are made righteous through faith in Jesus' perfect life, atoning death, and resurrection brought to Luther the crowning achievement of the Reformation—the rediscovery of the Gospel. And the world has not been the same since.

**PRAYER:** Father, I am so thankful that the Gospel is made clear in this verse. May I never forget that my relationship with You comes through faith in Jesus. Through His perfect life and substitutionary death, He gives His righteousness to me as a gift received by faith. Help me preach the Gospel to myself every day, remembering that I am a sinner saved by grace, and that I am a child of God only through faith in Jesus alone.

# S

*David found **strength**
in the LORD his God.*
1 Samuel 30:6

Sometimes we see the greatness of a man by the way he handles adversity. That is the way we should see David. With all the struggles he had before he became king, this verse follows perhaps the lowest point in his life. David had fled Saul, the current king of Israel, accompanied by only a small band of men, living day-to-day trying to survive.

So while David and his little army had left their camp to pursue their enemies, the Amalekites raided it, burned it to the ground, and took their wives and children as slaves. Upon returning to camp, David's men were so distraught that they considered stoning him. As terrible as these events were, having to deal with mutiny would have been the ultimate humiliation.

But what would David do? Stand up to the leader of the mutiny? Try some bold plan of rescue? Commit suicide?

1 Samuel 30:6 simply says, *"David found strength in the Lord his God."* He did not look to himself for answers. He did not make some well-crafted plan, nor some bold confrontation with the leaders of the mutiny. David prayed! He went directly to the Lord to deal with his own sense of loss, his own fear, his own feelings of inadequacy, or his own situation of loneliness.

What a great example for us all in times of severe testing. May our first response in a crisis be to look to God and find strength for the situation, that only He can give.

**PRAYER:** Father, I may never have a crisis as intense as David's. But I suspect I will have moments when everything around me seems to be falling apart. May I remember Your promise to never leave me or forsake me. Bring to my mind David's example that You should be the One I look to first for strength.

# T

*__Trust__ in the LORD with all your heart and lean
not on your own understanding; in all your ways
acknowledge him, and he will make your paths straight.*
Proverbs 3: 5–6

My wife and I have always made a big deal out of each of our three sons' birthdays. It is a day to give praise to God for the gift they are to us and celebrate their life. My wife prepares their favorite meal, and I offer a prayer on their behalf, giving thanks for them and asking for God's blessing upon them in the coming year.

Also, when they were young, I would read to them Proverbs 3:1–6. Verse 1 begins with, *"My son, do not forget my teaching, but keep my commands in your heart."*

The commands are summarized in our memory verse for today. Verses 5 and 6 state God's covenantal promises and our covenantal responsibilities. God promises to keep us with Him, guide us, protect us, and provide for us.

But we are to live by faith. We must rely on His Word for guidance, place our trust in what He says is best, and look to Him as our Lord. God's promises are true, but they come to us through the avenue of faith.

What a great verse for young people to hear, believe, and follow. What a great promise for believers of any age.

**PRAYER:** Gracious Lord, help me to memorize this amazing verse. It reminds me that so often, my first reaction is to trust in myself and forget that I have a Heavenly Father who always knows what is best. Increase my faith.

# U

*I do believe; help me*
*overcome my **unbelief**!*
Mark 9:24

As a father of three sons, I have a strong emotional connection to this dad in the Bible who needed help. His son had suffered for years, and he had brought his child to the disciples to be healed, but they couldn't do it.

Undeterred, the father brings his son to Jesus and says, *"But if you can do anything, have compassion on us and help us"* (9:22). We can only speculate about the tone of Jesus' answer, *"'If you can?' Everything is possible to him who believes"* (9:23).

To Jesus, building the father's trust as the first priority was even more important than healing the son's affliction. Jesus solicits a faith response before He will perform the healing. A faith that is weak but real is open to grow deeper. In response to the father's growing conviction and trust, Jesus heals the boy.

How often do we come to God like this man, thinking to

ourselves "If you can..." not "I know you can." Jesus honors the honesty of this man's little faith because though small, it is real. It is sincere. The man shows a growing faith, despite his doubt.

We would be blessed if we came to God in the spirit of this request. Rather than taking no for an answer due to our lack of persistence, we should be praying, *"Lord, I do believe. Help me overcome my unbelief."*

**PRAYER:** Lord Jesus, I probably cannot recall the number of times I have given up on my requests because my faith was weak. Bring to my mind this verse. Help it remind me that You are patient and gracious despite my weaknesses and that You will cause my faith to grow stronger as I trust in You.

# V

*This is the **victory** that has*
*overcome the world, even our faith.*
1 John 5:4

At the end of my college football career, I had the privilege of signing a professional NFL contract with the Washington Redskins (now the Washington Commanders). I had had some success as a three-year starter at quarterback at a Division II college, and somehow the Redskins took notice and sent one of their scouts to see me play. As a result, I received a free-agent contract with a bonus.

The real bonus, however, was meeting their head coach, the legendary Vince Lombardi. I attended the first day of Rookie Camp, and Coach Lombardi complimented me on my throwing ability. Later, all rookies were given thorough physicals by the team doctor.

Unfortunately, not having an agent and being naive to professional contracts, I shared with the doctor that I had played in college with a chronic back problem. After sharing this information, I was informed I had not passed the physical and was cut.

So how does this relate to our verse? Before going to Rookie Camp, I had read a book about Coach Lombardi's success coaching the Green Bay Packers.

Lombardi had a famous saying that goes: "Winning isn't everything; it's the only thing." The sports world will always remember Coach Lombardi's statement about the importance of winning.

It is noteworthy that John's letter to the churches has a similar theme. John uses the term "world" to refer to all forces that are in opposition to God's will. He writes with the goal that a Christian can have victory over the evil forces of the world, through the power of faith.

**PRAYER:** Lord, I know in this sinful world I will face ongoing temptations that go against Your good will for my life. Give me a faith so strong that I may be victorious despite the challenges that come my way.

# W

*__Without__ faith it is impossible to please God, for*
*anyone who comes to him must believe that he exists*
*and that he rewards those who earnestly seek him.*
Hebrews 11:6

I had the wonderful privilege of being trained in a presentation of the Gospel that I have used throughout my thirty-some years as a pastor. The training involved several days of learning and practicing a very specific outline.

The final night of instruction involved going out into the community in groups of three, two trainees and one experienced presenter. Before we left, we were told that once the presenter started sharing the Gospel outline, the rest of us were to keep silent.

We knocked on several random doors, and after the third attempt, a single woman in her twenties let us in. The presenter followed the outline perfectly. However, she sounded like she was reading from a script. And from her tone, she didn't seem to care at all about the person in front of her.

I have heard it said: "People don't care how much you know until they know how much you care."

This wise saying seems to apply to the Hebrews 11:6 definition of biblical faith. Not only does our faith require belief in the actual existence of God, but it also requires that we know that God is personal and caring and that He responds with generosity to those who put their trust in Him.

**PRAYER:** Lord, thank You for Your Word that teaches that I must believe in more than your mere existence to please You. May I speak of Your love, Your generosity and Your mercy wherever I go.

# X

*__E(x)cel__ in everything— in faith, in*
*speech, in knowledge, in complete*
*earnestness, and in your love.*
2 Corinthians 8:7

My dad excelled as a high school football coach. He always wanted his athletes to do their best, no matter what. He not only asked it from his players, but he modeled it in his own life.

I have always been thankful that he instilled that value in me. We may not be good at everything, but that does not mean we can't give our best at whatever we try: in our studies, sports, work, relationships, and more. An attitude of excellence can be applied in all aspects of life.

The Apostle Paul is saying something very similar here in terms of our spiritual life. We are to seek to do our best in the areas of faith, knowledge, earnestness, and love. God deserves our excellence in these areas, and pleasing our Heavenly Father should be our goal.

**PRAYER:** Lord, I will always say I believe in You, but sometimes I may not show it by what I do. I know that You want me to excel in these areas. Give me grace to do so.

# Y

*__Yea__, though I walk through the valley of the shadow
of death, I will fear no evil; for You are with me.*
Psalm 23:4 NKJV

When I met a dear old friend in a doctor's office as I was waiting
for a check-up, I was inspired by a story he shared with me. He told
me that several years earlier he began experiencing chest pains and
knew he was having a heart attack. While riding in the ambulance
on the way to the hospital, he was greatly comforted by repeating
this verse to himself. It sustained him through a time when he was
truly in the valley of the shadow of death.

But reciting this verse alone is not where we get our strength.
Reciting and believing in what it promises is what connects us
with God. He is the God of all comfort, who personally guarantees
He will walk beside us, even in the most difficult situations.
Memorizing this verse will enable us to sense God's presence in the
moments when we feel the need so intensely.

**PRAYER:** Heavenly Father, thank You for your promises. When I am frightened and feel threatened, or even facing death, may I look to You for Your calming and assuring presence. May fear never overcome me. May I know Your Word and believe it. When adversity comes, may I face it knowing You are right beside me.

# Z

*The **zeal** of the LORD Almighty*
*will accomplish this.*
Isaiah 37:32

People who lived through the COVID-19 pandemic will never forget it. It disrupted so many planned activities.

After graduation from college, our oldest grandson Blake had been engaged to his high school sweetheart, Kayla, for several months. They had planned their August wedding and reception at a gorgeous mansion with beautiful gardens.

But before their wedding date, the pandemic hit. Their wedding was scheduled at the peak of the COVID-19 outbreak and before there were any vaccines or treatments. The venue manager told them that if they had the wedding on the original date, the guest list could only be 25 instead of 125, and the cost would remain the same.

The only concession the venue offered was to have the wedding and reception for 125 guests on that date, one year later.

Some couples might have said, "Let's just live together anyway and get married in one year." But my grandson and his fiancée, in their zeal to please the Lord, would not do that.

Instead, Blake and Kayla had their wedding and reception on the original date in our backyard, with all twenty of their planned attendants and about twenty-five family members. By God's grace, no one came down with the virus, and they had a one-year anniversary wedding reenactment at their original venue.

Our verse for today resulted from God's promise to honor the faith of the great King Hezekiah, who would not surrender to the Assyrians. Hezekiah looked to God for his protection and would honor only Him. The people of Judah were saved because, as Isaiah predicted, *"The zeal of the LORD Almighty will accomplish this."*

~

**PRAYER**: Lord, You are zealous for Your people. May I have a real zeal to do what is right in Your eyes, for Jesus' sake.

# PART THREE
# WITNESSING

# WITNESSING

Christ's first instructions to His new followers in the first chapter of Mark were, "*Come after me and I will make you fishers of men.*" His last instructions on this earth to His disciples were, "*But you shall receive power, after the Holy Spirit comes upon you: and you shall be my witnesses in Jerusalem, and in Judea, and in Samaria, and unto the uttermost parts of the earth.*" Christ thus began and ended His ministry with the command to be witnesses and fishers of men!

—D. James Kennedy, *Evangelism Explosion*, p. 2

Note: All the Scripture verses that are used in the evangelism course "Evangelism Explosion III," by D. James Kennedy, are included in this section.

## List of Witnessing Verses

"**All** have sinned and fall short of the glory of God."
Romans 3:23

"**Be** perfect, therefore, as your heavenly Father is perfect."
Matthew 5:48

"**Come** to me, all who are weary and burdened, and I will give you rest."
Matthew 11:28

"You believe that there is one God. Good! Even the **demons** believe that—and shudder."
James 2:19

"The gift of God is **eternal** life in Christ Jesus our Lord."
Romans 6:23

"**For** it is by grace you have been saved, through faith-and this not from yourselves, it is the gift of God, not by works, so that no one can boast."
Ephesians 2:8–9

"**God** so loved the world that he gave his one and only Son, that whoever believes in him shall not perish but have eternal life."
John 3:16

"**He** himself bore our sins in his body on the tree, so that we might die to sins and live for righteousness; by his wounds you have been healed."
1 Peter 2:24

"**It** is finished."
John 19:30

"**Jesus** answered, "The work of God is this: to believe in the one he has sent."
John 6:29

"All men will **know** that you are my disciples if you love one another."
John 13:34

"God is **love**."
1 John 4:16

"Thomas said to him, "**My** Lord and my God!""
John 20:28

"**Now** this is eternal life: that they may know you, the only true God, and Jesus Christ, whom you have sent."
John 17:3

"Believe **on** the Lord Jesus Christ, and you will be saved."
Acts 16:31 NKJV

"I am not ashamed of the gospel, because it is the **power** of God for the salvation of everyone who believes."
Romans 1:6

"For since the creation of the world God's invisible **qualities**—his eternal power and divine nature have been clearly seen, being understood from what has been made, so that men are without excuse."
Romans 1:20

"For as far as the east is from the west, so far has he **removed** our transgressions from us."
Psalm 103:12

"If you confess with your mouth, "Jesus is Lord," and believe in your heart that God raised him from the dead, you will be **saved**."
Romans 10:9

"I write these **things** to you who believe in the name of the Son of God so that you may know that you have eternal life."
1 John 5:13

"The Word became flesh and lived for a while among **us**."
John 1:14

"I stand at the door and knock. If anyone hears my **voice** and opens the door, I will go in and eat with him, and he with me."
Revelation 3:20

"**We** all, like sheep, have gone astray, each of us has turned to his own way; and the LORD has laid on him the iniquity of us all."
Isaiah 53:6

"Set an **e(x)ample** for the believers in speech, in life, in love, in faith and in purity."
1 Timothy 4:12

"**Yet** to all who received him, to those who believed in his name, he gave the right to become children of God."
John 1:12

"Never be lacking in **zeal**, but keep your spiritual fervor, serving the Lord."
Romans 12:11

# A

*__All__ have sinned and fall short of the glory of God.*
Romans 3:23

Being of the Baby Boomer generation, I grew up in a time when almost everyone in America had some type of religious affiliation. In the various methods of evangelism, discussing the issue of being a sinner was fairly well understood. For my generation, a respect for the Bible and the Ten Commandments was the cultural norm. When you did what was wrong in God's eyes, it was called sin, and you were accountable to God for it.

There has been a profound shift in our culture to what is often given the label Post-truth. No longer are the Bible and Christian ethics the dominant cultural standard. In the public square, freedom from religion is the prevailing attitude of the society we now live in.

But God's Word has not changed. It reflects the character of the sovereign God who created us and to whom we will all one day stand before and be judged. Witnessing using the word sin is harder today. To a Post-truth culture whose highest value is individual freedom, answering to a God whose standard is His own righteous character requires a methodology that goes beyond quoting Scripture as authoritative.

Regardless of the change in cultural norms, the truth of Romans 3:23 is as important today as it ever was. People are sinners and unless they believe in Jesus as their sinless substitute, they will have to face God's righteous judgment.

**PRAYER:** Father, Your Word is true whether the culture agrees or not. Help me pray for and be a witness to a generation that needs Jesus as their Savior.

# B

*__Be__ perfect, therefore, as your heavenly Father is perfect.*
Matthew 5:48

As a child growing up, my image of God was that of a grandfather figure with a long white beard, who was kind-hearted and turned a blind eye to everyone's sin. Sin was no big deal. The grandfather-in-the-sky God would not really punish anyone but just let things slide. But I had not read the Bible, nor had I heard any teaching on the righteous judgment of God.

That God is perfect is one of the most significant attributes that we can understand about Him. He is perfect in love, perfect in righteousness, perfect in wisdom, perfect in justice, perfect in patience, etc. All moral qualities find their highest standard and completeness in the Lord.

Mankind's tendency is to try to make God into our own image. Understanding that God must be perfectly just, however, is vital in comprehending our need for a Savior. Our sin, the result of our moral imperfection, keeps us from fellowship with the Lord.

Habakkuk 1:13 says: *"Your eyes are too pure to look on evil; you cannot tolerate wrong."* That is why we need a mediator. Jesus' death on the cross created a bridge for sinners to have a relationship with a Holy God. And because Christ lived a perfect life, His righteousness is imputed to us. It is put on our account. As a result, God sees us perfect "in Christ" (Romans 5:17).

**PRAYER:** Heavenly Father, my natural tendency is to try to make You into my image. But your Word reminds me that You are perfect, and I am not. I am thankful that being in Jesus, You see me clothed in His righteousness.

# C

*__Come__ to me, all who are weary and*
*burdened, and I will give you rest.*
Matthew 11:28

The great evangelist Billy Graham's most influential book was one of his earliest. In that book entitled *Peace With God*, he makes it emphatically clear that peace with God is every person's greatest need. And the only way that can happen is through accepting Jesus' invitation to be their Savior.

Matthew 11:28 is one of those great invitations. Jesus invites "all," to come to Him in faith and receive rest. Rest is another way of saying, "peace with God."

Jesus is aware that people may think that because they have struggles, they have nothing to offer Him. But that is what is so special about the invitation. Jesus takes the initiative to invite people with difficulties, with heartache and with a sinful lifestyle, to come to Him and receive the answer to the greatest need in their soul. Rest is a settled contentment, a freedom from excess concerns, a refuge in a storm, a firm place to stand. But most of all, it is a restored relationship with God that gives us eternal peace.

**PRAYER:** Lord, too many times I have handled my worry and stress by withdrawing. Let me hear You again invite me into Your presence to share my concerns and find the kind of rest only You can provide.

# D

*You believe that there is one God. Good!*
*Even the **demons** believe that—and shudder.*
James 2:19

One of the first times I watched a video with theologian and author R.C. Sproul, he made the statement, "O you believe in God? That qualifies you at least to be a demon." I was a bit shocked.

In my limited knowledge of the Bible, I had not grasped the significance of what was being said in James 2:19. Sproul's rather cryptic remark jarred me into understanding that, just because someone believes God exists doesn't mean that they are trusting Him for anything. "Saving faith" is much more than agreeing that there is a God. By saying *"even the demons believe and shudder,"* we are reminded that a person can have a belief in the historicity of Jesus but not have saving faith.

Our "W" Faith verse is so instructive here. It says, *"Without faith it is impossible to please God, for anyone who comes to him must believe he exits and rewards those who earnestly seek him."* Coming to God and knowing He rewards our faith is the very opposite of how the demons react to Him. Intellectual assent is not the faith that results in blessings from God.

**PRAYER:** Dear Lord, thank You for giving me a faith that goes deeper than just intellectual assent. May You give me discernment, so I can know who needs to hear about Your saving work for sinners.

# E

*The gift of God is **eternal** life in*
*Christ Jesus our Lord.*
Romans 6:23

Until I was twenty- eight years old, I had always believed that getting into heaven was something you had to constantly work for and could never be assured of achieving.

Eternal life—life without end, everlasting fellowship with God —is a gift. That means it cannot be earned or deserved, but only received. This is an important reminder that external striving and all work-related efforts cannot be the source of eternal life.

This new life with God comes to us through faith in a person, Jesus Christ, the incarnate Son of God. His sacrificing His life in our place is a result of God's grace. No amount of our striving could work off our debt. This payment is offered freely and is to be received by faith alone.

**PRAYER:** Heavenly Father, there is no gift as great as eternal life. May I live each day remembering that knowing You is the result of your loving grace, something that I could never earn or deserve.

# F

*__For__ it is by grace you have been saved, through faith*
*—and this not from yourselves, it is the gift of God—*
*not by works, so that no one can boast.*
Ephesians 2:8–9

I had a dear friend named Dave who grew up in a Plymouth Brethren congregation in Baltimore City. All ages met together in one room where there were Scripture verses written all over the walls. One of the verses on the front wall was Ephesians 2:8–9.

The practice at their meeting was to go around the room and ask each person to recite a passage from memory. Young Dave didn't know any verses by heart, so whenever it was his turn to recite a verse, he would simply glance up front and read Ephesians 2:8–9. He got called on regularly and routinely would read these same two verses. But after doing this numerous times, he came to understand and believe in his heart the deep meaning of these words. The truth of this passage became personal, and he believed that Jesus had died for his sins and that he was truly saved. Dave went on as an adult to become an elder in the church and serve the Lord faithfully all his life.

There may be no place in the Bible where the message of salvation is more clearly summarized than in these two verses. Salvation is by grace alone through faith alone in Christ alone. It is an unmerited favor. If there is any question that works contribute to a believer's eternal destiny, the last phrase of this passage clearly settles that argument. There can be no boasting about our efforts. The fact that salvation is completely the result of a gift means that we get no credit. It is all the result of God's amazing grace.

**PRAYER:** Heavenly Father, whenever I begin to have feelings of self-righteousness or see myself as superior to unbelievers, may the Holy Spirit bring this verse to my mind. May I never boast of anything that I have done to merit my sins to be forgiven and receive eternal life. All glory goes to Jesus.

# G

***God*** *so loved the world that he gave his*
*one and only Son, that whoever believes*
*in him shall not perish but have eternal life.*
John 3:16

Until I heard the explanation of this verse from two members of a
new church my wife and I had just visited, it meant little to me.
For the first twenty-eight years of my life, I had always believed you
had to work your way to heaven and that you could have no real
assurance in your salvation. But on a September night in 1976, two
visitors from that church shared that heaven was a free gift. And
although all had sinned and fallen short of the glory of God, Jesus
Christ had died on the cross to purchase a place for me in heaven.

To me, Jesus had been little more than an example of how I
should live in order to earn my way to heaven. But when one of the
men quoted John 3:16, and he came to the phrase, *"whoever*
*believes in him shall not perish but have eternal life,"* it was like a
light bulb went off in my head. The "Him" of that verse was not

some generic God as I had imagined. The "Him" of that verse was Jesus. Jesus had come to earth to pay for my sins. My sins! He was my Savior, and I owed my life to Him.

When I was asked, "Does this make sense to you? I said, "Yes!" Moments later, I prayed to God, asking that my sins be forgiven and Jesus to come into my life and be my Savior and Lord. From that point on my life was changed forever.

**PRAYER:** Dear Jesus, thank You for giving words that explain what You did for me by dying on the cross. May this well-known verse be a constant reminder of Your love, Your sacrifice, and the gift of life You have given to me.

# H

*__He__ himself bore our sins in his body on the tree,
so that we might die to sins and live for
righteousness; by his wounds you have been healed.*
1 Peter 2:24

At Covenant of Grace Church, we celebrated the Lord's supper once a month during the morning services. While the elements were being passed, it was my practice to recite Scripture. One of my favorites was this verse. At the Lord's Supper, we remember Jesus' death. But in partaking of the elements, we should also remember that for the believer, His death brings healing in a very significant way.

But how does Jesus' death on the cross bring us healing? The answer is that it heals us from the sickness called "sin." At His crucifixion, Jesus took our sins upon His shoulders and paid the penalty due for our transgressions against God.

With this new life, we get a new power. Out of love for Christ and gratitude for His sacrifice, we have a newfound desire to turn away from our sinful actions and attitudes. In addition, as we turn from sin, we also have a passion to follow the teachings of Christ. This is the healthy life that God wants us to live.

**PRAYER:** Dear Jesus, You are the great physician. Thank You for healing me from the power of sin and giving me a new way of living. May I demonstrate the reality of my new life in You through my actions each day.

# I

*__It__ is finished.*
John 19:30

When asked, "What is the shortest sentence in the Bible?", most people who know the Bible will routinely answer, "Jesus wept," referring to John 11:32. And among translations in English, that would be correct.

But as many people know, the New Testament was originally written in the Greek language and the shortest sentence in the original is this verse, John 19:20. In the Greek Bible the sentence we know as *"It is finished"* is just one word—*tetelestai*.

The word itself is in the Greek tense that involves past, present, and future simultaneously. The word *tetelestai* would have the sense in English of "it is finished for the past, present, and future."

It is important to note that Jesus did not say "I am finished," or "I am about to die." He cried out, *"It is finished!"*

What is the "it" that Jesus is referring to? It is none other than the work of redemption the Father sent Him to earth to accomplish. It is His coming to live a perfect life and to die as the perfect sacrifice for sin and be raised from the dead so that we might have everlasting life.

Cults come and go and seek to teach that something must be added to the work of Jesus for salvation. But Jesus' statement, *"It is finished,"* is the clear reminder that all that was needed to provide for eternal life was completed by Him on the cross. The classic hymn says it well. "Jesus paid it all, all to Him I owe." Jesus' words declare unmistakably that nothing needs to be added, the debt has been paid. All we are to do is receive His finished work by faith.

**PRAYER:** Dear Jesus, may your words, *"It is finished,"* remind me that I can add nothing to what you accomplished on the cross. May I rest in the fact that what You did completed all the righteous requirements of God for my salvation.

# J

*__Jesus__ answered, "The work of God is*
*this: to believe in the one he has sent."*
John 6:29

My wife and I love our three sons very much. If asked "Would you do anything for your children?" our quick response would be, "Of course!" But given a few moments to think about the question, we should say: "Of course not! We wouldn't lie for our kids, cheat, or steal for them." Something of a much less serious nature—we would never do their homework for them. We believed their ability to find the answer for themselves was much more important than being spoon-fed by us.

I believe Jesus is doing something similar here. When He was confronted by skeptics about who He was and what it was His Father sent Him to do, He often used phrases that would confound (John 6:29). Here is Jesus' response to a group of critics who asked the wrong-minded question: *"What must we do to do the works God requires?"* (John 6:28) Jesus' answer seems contradictory. Believing in Him is not a work at all but a matter of faith. Jesus used this answer as He used parables, to cause people to think more deeply.

There are many people today who see Christianity as a religion of works. They think that to be a Christian you must do this or do that. Jesus' answer is as relevant today as it was in the first century. Working for salvation is sinful man's natural fallback position. The apostle Paul explains it explicitly in Romans 4:5 when he says, *"to the man who does not work, but trusts God who justifies the wicked, his faith is credited as righteousness."* Our relationship with God is through faith, not works.

**PRAYER:** Dear Jesus, there is often a subtle tendency for me to think that I can earn my salvation by what I do, or how I behave. Remind me that my salvation comes by trusting in You alone.

# K

*All men will **know** that you are
my disciples if you love one another.*
John 13: 35

I have a close friend who was very good at sharing his faith at work. One of his problems, however, was that one of his co-workers, who was very outspoken about her faith, was rude to her fellow workers. When my friend attempted to witness, the previous less-than-kind actions of this woman tended to undermine what he was trying to accomplish.

Throughout His ministry, Jesus knew that many people would not understand that He represented the Father's love. But though people might doubt Him, if they saw the disciples loving and caring for each other, they could not deny that somehow Jesus' example made a difference.

You can be skeptical of one's words, but when love is demonstrated through actions, it is hard to deny that something is behind it. Love between Christians, especially love in congregations, is a powerful testimony that Jesus makes a difference in peoples' lives. Some may wonder about it, but they will have a hard time arguing it away.

**PRAYER:** Dear Jesus, help me to remember that I can be a witness for You by loving my brothers and sisters in the Lord. Let my love toward the fellow believers in my church be so obvious that people would want what we have.

# L

*God is **love**.*
1 John 4:16

In one of my all-time favorite movies, *Friendly Persuasion*, during a silent time in their Quaker Meeting, a young Quaker boy blurts out the verse, "God is love!" Instead of loving approval for his exclamation of such an important truth, he receives disapproving glares from all the stern-faced elders in the Meeting. The hypocrisy of their response is evident to all watching the film.

John says twice in his epistle, *"God is love"* (1 John 4:8, 4:16). This is one of the most profound, all-encompassing statements in the Bible. Love is not all that God is, but it is a marvelous summary of his character. To say that God is love means that His love finds expression in everything He says or does.

Love is an exercise of God's goodness toward sinners whereby, having concern for our welfare, He has given His Son to be our Savior. Because of God's love, He enables us to know Him and enjoy Him in a covenant relationship. Through our believing, and

God's Holy Spirit dwelling in us, we have a new ability to love like God and share His love with others.

**PRAYER:** Gracious and loving God, You have loved me, not because I have deserved it, but because it is something that flows from Your heart. May Your love flow from my heart as well.

# M

*Thomas said to him, "__My__ Lord and my God!"*
John 20:28

From the very first days following the resurrection of Jesus, there have been those who have tried to disprove its reality. Arguments by many critics are absurd simply because they lack any reasonable standard of proof. I remember when I was in college, there was a book entitled *The Passover Plot* in our campus bookstore. It was based on the premise that Jesus' resurrection was a well-orchestrated hoax devised by His disciples.

The critical argument that angers me the most is the claim that Jesus was unaware that He was the Son of God. The Gospel of John is written to prove that Jesus was very much aware that He was the Messiah. All the "I am" passages should be adequate proof to any honest seeker of truth.

But one irrefutable proof is here in the testimony of "Doubting Thomas." Thomas discredits all who say that the disciples did not acknowledge Jesus' divinity. After a time of skepticism, from which Thomas gets his nickname, Doubting Thomas, he gives his personal testimony to the deity of Christ with his spontaneous declaration, "My Lord and my God."

**PRAYER:** Dear Jesus, the mystery of Your incarnation is great. But I have, in Your Word, clear teaching that, although Your divinity was veiled in flesh for a time, You are Lord and God. May the desire of my heart be to bow down before You and know the truth of Thomas' declaration, that You are my Lord and my God.

# N

*__Now__ this is eternal life: that they may know you, the only true God, and Jesus Christ, whom you have sent.*
John 17:3

Growing up in the church, I always believed in heaven and the concept of eternal life. But my understanding of eternal life was that it referred to a future existence. You don't have eternal life until you die and go to heaven.

But that is not what Jesus teaches. Here, He makes it abundantly clear that eternal life is a present relationship with God. It is not an experience in the distant future. Eternal life comes immediately upon receiving Jesus Christ as Savior and Lord. By having Him in our life we know the true God—the gracious and forgiving God who sent His Son to die for us.

When we die a physical death, eternal life doesn't begin, we merely make a transition from earthly life to a life in heaven that grows richer and richer in knowing and enjoying God.

**PRAYER:** Dear Jesus, when You came into my life, You gave me a new relationship and a wonderful future. May I understand that eternal life is now. And may I look forward to an even greater intimacy with You in the future.

# O

*Believe **on** the Lord Jesus Christ,
and you will be saved.*
Acts 16:31 NKJV

One of the great demonstrations of what saving faith is like is the "empty chair" illustration as taught by EE III International. An empty chair is placed in the center of the room representing Jesus. The presenter asks the person they are sharing the Gospel with if they see the chair.

Then they are asked, "Do you believe it exists?" After they answer yes, the question that follows is: "Do you believe it would hold you if you sat in it?" Again, after another "Yes" answer, the next question is, "How can you prove it?" The answer again that is obvious is, "By sitting on it."

The dramatic illustration to make a personal decision comes when the presenter says, "Have you ever gotten out of your own chair and placed your trust in Jesus Christ for eternal life?" The person is then asked to demonstrate transferring their trust from themselves to Jesus by getting out of their chair and then sitting in the empty chair.

This presentation clearly visualizes what saving faith truly is. It involves transferring our trust from the perceived merit of our own good deeds and relying on Jesus Christ alone for our salvation.

**PRAYER:** Heavenly Father, help me to remember that eternal life is not trusting in myself or merely believing You exist, but by transferring my trust to Jesus and relying solely on His life, death, and resurrection to be the perfect sacrifice for my sins.

# P

*I am not ashamed of the gospel,
because it is the **power** of God for
the salvation of everyone who believes.*
Romans 1:16

Up until 1867, the most powerful explosive was a chemical called nitroglycerin. The major problem, however, was that it was very unstable, and a mere shake of the volatile chemical could create a deadly explosion. It was not until Swedish physicist Alfred Noble combined it with diatomaceous earth and a blasting cap that it became safe enough to be used commercially. Patented in 1867, it was originally sold as Noble's Blasting Powder. But Noble soon changed the name using the Ancient Greek word for power, *dynamis*. And so, it has been known ever since as dynamite.

The Apostle Paul uses the Greek word *dynamis* to describe the incredible life-giving effect of the good news of Jesus Christ, best summarized by the word "Gospel." Paul intends to take that message to the great city of Rome. He uses somewhat ironic language when he declares he is not "ashamed" of the gospel. On the contrary, he is excited and can hardly wait to get to Rome because he knows that the gospel contains the only message that can powerfully change lives.

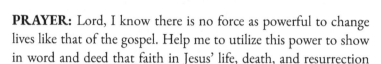

**PRAYER:** Lord, I know there is no force as powerful to change lives like that of the gospel. Help me to utilize this power to show in word and deed that faith in Jesus' life, death, and resurrection can transform lives.

# Q

*For since the creation of the world God's invisible **qualities**—his eternal power and divine nature—have been clearly seen, being understood from what has been made, so that men are without excuse.*
Romans 1:20

Over my many years as a pastor, it was always exciting to share the good news of Jesus Christ with a seeker. By the term "seeker," I mean someone who shows genuine interest in the Gospel. Although they are not yet a believer, they have questions to which they sincerely want answers.

For example, one of the questions that frequently comes up goes something like this: "What about the people who have never heard about Jesus? It does not seem fair for God to send them to hell if they have never heard?"

Whether or not you can memorize this long verse, knowing its content is crucial in answering this very frequent question. The point that Paul is making is that everyone knows deep down in their heart that there is a God. Nature itself is a revelation to all that there is a Creator God.

To be a professing atheist requires someone to intentionally suppress the revelation of the existence of God they already have. This suppression does not excuse the person from having to face the fact that because God created them, they have to answer to Him. As Romans 1:20 points out, ignorance is not an excuse.

**PRAYER:** Creator God, You have made the universe so that everyone can see Your power and majesty. I am grateful that You have given me new eyes through which I can give You praise for all the grandeur of Your creation I see.

# R

*As far as the east is from the west, so far has he **removed** our transgressions from us.*
Psalm 103:12

Several years ago, my wife and I were thinking of selling our two-story colonial and moving into a compact rancher. To prepare for the sale, we had a solid off-white carpet installed throughout our entire second floor.

Several days after the installation, I accidentally tracked some of my wife's artist oil paint onto the new carpet. I immediately leaped into action, pouring paint thinner onto a rag and rubbing with all my might. Unfortunately, I only made matters worse. My efforts simply spread the paint into a larger and larger area.

In desperation, I got on the Internet, where I learned that the secret to removing oil paint from carpet requires a blotting technique. So, following this method, I slowly and methodically used paint thinner and dozens of clean paper towels to blot the spot.

The paper towels absorbed the paint, and amazingly, the stains were gone.

To have stain removed is also necessary for us to have fellowship with a holy God. Psalm 103:12 tells us our sin is removed as far as the mind can conceive. What a comforting truth. A vital word in this verse, however, is the simple pronoun "he." He, of course, refers to God.

In Psalm 51 David asks God to *"blot out my transgressions."* David knows to be restored to fellowship, God must remove the stain. And just like paint-thinner-soaked paper towels are needed to remove paint from a carpet, so God had to provide a way to remove the stain of sin from us. God did that by sending His Son to bear our sins in His body on the cross. (1 Peter 2:24). We could say that when Jesus took our sins upon Himself, He blotted out our sin and absorbed them into Himself so we could stand clean in the presence of a holy God.

~

**Prayer:** Lord Jesus, may I never forget that on the cross you bore my sins, you blotted out all my stain so I could be clean in the presence of God for all eternity,

# S

*If you confess with your mouth, "Jesus
is Lord," and believe in your heart that God
raised him from the dead, you will be __saved__.*
Romans 10:9

As a preacher, I have never been fond of using the word "saved" in
my sermons on Sunday mornings even though it is biblical. The
word "saved" however, begs the question: Saved from what? Obviously, more information needs to follow for those who are unfa-
miliar with this biblical term.

The answer to the question is two-fold: 1) Saved to an eternal
life with God and 2) saved from eternal separation from God in
hell.

Our memory verse teaches two other chief aspects of our confidence in eternal life. We should express with a public profession in
some way our faith in Jesus. Also, we need to proclaim our conviction that He rose from the dead. This statement declares that we

believe we are saved from God's wrath and saved to resurrection life.

**PRAYER:** Heavenly Father, thank You that your Word gives me clear assurance of my salvation. May I seek to share my faith in word and deed and remember what I am saved "from" and saved "to."

T

*I write* these ***things*** *to you who believe in the name of the Son of God so that you may know that you have eternal life.*
1 John 5:13

When I was eight years old, my dear paternal grandfather died of pancreatic cancer. My mother later told me that the night before he died, he stated to my grandmother, that he was not sure he was going to heaven. Knowing that has been grievous to me, especially because he was an ordained Protestant minister. What is more disturbing to me was my grandmother's response to his concern. She did not comfort him with the gospel. Instead, she said, "But George, you've lived a good life."

Throughout Christian history, there have been preachers and denominations that teach that you cannot know for sure that you are going to heaven. This view is a denial of what is clearly stated in our passage of Scripture for today.

1 John is written to those who have fellowship *"with the Father and with his Son, Jesus Christ."* (1 John 1:3) The context clearly

shows that this is not talking about some universal doctrine of salvation. But it is written to those who have put their trust in Jesus as Savior and Lord. It is John's desire that believers have the assurance that they are safe and secure in Jesus through faith. Inspired writers guided by the Holy Spirit have written a principle that gives believers confidence, joy, and hope.

**PRAYER**: Father, I am so grateful that the Scriptures clearly state that those who have Jesus in their heart, are eternally secure. Thank you that I have your Word, not only written in my inner being but also on the printed page.

# U

*The Word became flesh and lived*
*for a while among __us__.*
John 1:14

When I was five years old, my mother went to work full-time as an elementary-school music teacher, and my maternal grandparents took care of me during the day. My grandfather was a retired pastor, and I remember him teaching me to memorize my very first Bible verse. It was John 1:1 and it goes, *"In the beginning was the Word and the Word was with God, and the Word was God."*

I have never regretted him encouraging me to do this. But looking back, I wish he had also taught me verse 14 of that chapter because I had no idea that John 1:1 was actually referring to Jesus, the incarnate Son of God.

Even now, I can't begin to fully explain the enormity of the significance of this verse. But two things are made apparent. First, that the second person of the Trinity, the Son of God, condescended to leave heaven and put on flesh and live in a human body.

And secondly, that having taken on our full humanity, He was willing to live as one of us, even living among us.

The degree of humility and love demonstrated in the incarnation of Jesus Christ is truly beyond comprehension. Yet, this proves, as is so often the case, that our God is much greater, much more mysterious, much more gracious and loving than our minds could ever conceive.

**PRAYER:** Dear Jesus, words could never express my thankfulness for Your condescending love. That You would leave the riches of heaven to bring about my salvation is overwhelming. Although I cannot fully understand why You loved me so much, I believe it and give You the praise.

# V

*I stand at the door and knock. If anyone hears my **voice** and opens the door, I will go in and eat with him, and he with me.*
Revelation 3:20

Some years ago, our church sent me and my wife to Morocco on a mission trip. One of the goals was to see firsthand the challenges that missionaries face in a non-Christian Third World country. Another goal was to encourage them in the Word and bring them some useful items.

One of the things we learned in Morocco was that in many ways it was culturally similar to 1st-century Israel, especially in the area of hospitality. Sharing mint tea was an honored custom.

My wife in particular, was invited into numerous homes where she was expected to drink at least three glasses of heavily sweetened mint tea. (Note: To this day my wife cannot force herself to drink mint tea).

Tea drinking aside, whenever she entered someone's home, she was treated as a deeply honored guest. To receive Jesus into your home, as today's verse describes is a visual illustration of this time-honored custom.

But Revelation 3:20 can also be used in evangelism. Encouraging someone to open the door in response to Jesus' knocking is clearly a picture of personally receiving Him into your life. But it is also significant to see that Jesus is the one who initiates the relationship.

**PRAYER:** Dear Jesus, I am so thankful that You pursued a relationship with me. I give You all the praise for enabling me to hear Your voice and open the door.

# W

*__We__ all, like sheep, have gone astray,*
*each of us has turned to his own way; and*
*the LORD has laid on him the iniquity of us all.*
Isaiah 53:6

In the EE III outline, the substitutionary death of Jesus in this verse is used powerfully with a simple illustration using just your two hands. In the illustration of the substitutionary sacrifice of Jesus dying on the cross for our sins in the EE III International outline, this verse is used powerfully with a simple illustration using just your two hands. First, the presenter takes a book, places it in one hand, and describes it as the record book of your sins. The empty hand represents Jesus. When the presenter quotes Isaiah 53:6 and comes to the words "laid on him," the presenter moves the book from the hand representing yourself, to the empty hand representing Jesus.

This provides a visual illustration that by placing our sins on

Jesus, He takes our sins on Himself. Our empty hand demonstrates that our sins have now been removed.

No verse in Scripture describes the substitutionary sacrifice for our sins by Jesus better than this one. It states the reality that every person is a sinner. No one is exempt from the sinful nature that causes us to rebel against God. But the good news, the wonderful message of the gospel, is that God has made a way for us to be freed from the debt we owe. God the Father placed our sin on God the Son as a guilt offering, so that a satisfactory payment could be made. He was the substitute who took our sin upon Himself.

**PRAYER:** Jesus, I will never be able to repay you for what you have done for me. Thank You for taking my sins upon yourself so I could be free.

# X

*Set an **e(x)ample** for the believers in speech,
in life, in love, in faith and in purity.*
1 Timothy 4:12

Within three years of accepting Jesus as my Savior, my family and I had moved from Maryland to attend seminary in St. Louis, Missouri. One of the reasons I was able to make that decision so early in my Christian life was because God placed a very special man in my life to disciple me, Mike Smelser, my brother-in law. Mike had come to personal faith in Christ a few years before and had himself, been extensively discipled in a wonderful church in Virginia Beach, while he worked in Norfolk as a Secret Service Agent.

In the providence of God, Mike was transferred to the Washington, D.C. office right at the time of my conversion. Unable to quickly sell their house in Virginia Beach, Mike stayed during the week with our in-laws and commuted from Finksburg, Maryland, to D.C.

He would then go back to Virginia Beach on the weekends. While staying with our in-laws, Mike began a Bible study. I had never been in a Bible study before, so it was all new to me. Thankfully, after the Bible study was over, Mike would stay up into the wee hours of the morning, explaining the truths of the scriptures to me. Observing his love for the scriptures, I also developed a deep, love for God's Word.

I had known Mike before he was a Christian and could see how God had transformed his life. He modeled to me that a man I had known as a tremendous athlete and fearless in a dangerous job, could also be a man of great faith. He was for me what Barnabas had been to Paul, a profound example and encourager.

**PRAYER:** Lord, thank You for bringing godly people into my life who can effectively teach Your Word and show me how to live by their example.

# Y

*__Yet__ to all who received him, to those who believed in his name, he gave the right to become children of God.*
John 1:12

A simple way to illustrate this verse's truth when sharing your faith with a seeker is: take a pen and tell the person that you sincerely want to give it to them as a gift. Hold out the pen toward them and say: "This pen isn't yours until you..." And they will undoubtedly say: "Take it." (After they take the pen be sure and make them keep it.)

Of the many verses in the Bible that describe the need for saving faith to be personal, this may be the clearest, most direct one of all. Salvation through faith in Jesus is sincerely offered to all. But in order for it to become yours, it must be received. It must be grasped, taken in, and believed to be something you personally possess. A gift is offered freely, but it can be ignored or even refused. To receive Jesus as your Savior means to put your trust fully in Him for eternal life. It is more than agreeing to certain facts. It includes a personal decision to take God's offer of salvation as your own.

**PRAYER:** Father, I understand that salvation is a free gift that must be received personally. Thank You for this wonderful verse that reminds me so clearly that I am a child of God because I have personally trusted in Jesus.

# Z

*Never be lacking in **zeal**, but keep
your spiritual fervor, serving the Lord.*
Romans 12:11

When I tell people I pastored one church for thirty-nine years, some seem amazed. But I also wonder if they are thinking something else. On one hand, they may be impressed (I get the same reaction when I tell non-religious people I have been married to the same woman for over 55 years). But on the other hand, perhaps they are wondering, "How could he possibly stay at one church and not burn out?"

Pastoral ministry can be very draining at times, and burnout is a potential possibility. One of the discouraging parts of doing ministry is the apparent lack of success. A way of overcoming this form of discouragement is to focus on being faithful to what you feel God has called you to do. No pastor or lay leader is truly responsible for the results. Only God can bring about a good outcome. But if in your heart you believe you are being faithful and doing God's will, you can be encouraged. And with that in the forefront of your mind, you can keep a spiritual fervor.

**PRAYER:** Lord Jesus, I confess at times I feel my zeal is not what it should be. I get tired and discouraged. May I fix my eyes on You and focus on being faithful.

# Part Four
# Worship

# WORSHIP

Worship is homage, adoration. It is not primarily for ourselves, but for the One we seek to honor. We worship for His pleasure foremost and find our greatest pleasure in pleasing Him. Worship must therefore be God-centered and Christ-centered. It must be focused on the covenant Lord.

John M. Frame, *Worship in Spirit and Truth*, p. 4

## LIST OF WORSHIP VERSES

"**As** the deer pants for streams of water, so my soul pants for you, O God."
Psalm 42:1

"**Be** still, and know that I am God."
Psalm 46:10

"**Come,** let us sing for joy to the LORD; let us shout aloud to the Rock of our salvation."
Psalm 95:1

"This is the **day** the LORD has made; let us rejoice and be glad in it."
Psalm 118:24

"His love **endures** forever."
Psalm 136:1

"Let us **fix** our eyes on Jesus, the author and perfecter of our faith."
Hebrews 12:4

"Ascribe to the LORD the **glory** due his name."
Psalm 29:2

"**How** great the love the Father has lavished on us, that we should be called children of God. And that is what we are."
1 John 3:1

"**If** we confess our sins, he is faithful and just and will

forgive us our sins and purify us from all unrighteousness."
1 John 1:9

"Through **Jesus,** therefore, let us continually offer to God a sacrifice of praise-the fruit of lips that confess his name."
Hebrews 13:15

"Your **kingdom** is an everlasting kingdom and your dominion endures through all generations."
Psalm 145:13

"The **LORD** is compassionate and gracious, slow to anger and rich in love."
Psalm 145:8

"God is spirit, and his worshippers **must** worship in spirit and in truth."
John 4:24

"Let us **not** give up meeting together as some are in the habit of doing."
Hebrews 10:25

"**O**, LORD, our Lord, how majestic is your name in all the earth!"
Psalm 8:1

"**Praise** be to the God and Father of our Lord Jesus Christ!
"
1 Peter 1:4

"Come with me by yourselves to a **quiet** place and get some rest."
Mark 6:31

"What do you have that you did not **receive**?"
1 Corinthians 4:7

"**Sing** to the LORD a new song."
Psalm 96:1

"**This** is love: not that we loved God, but that he loved us and sent his son as an atoning sacrifice for our sins."
1 John 4:10

"Have mercy on me, O God, according to your **unfailing** love."
Psalm 51:1

"Therefore, I urge you, brothers, in **view** of God's mercy, to offer your bodies as living sacrifices."
Romans 12:1

"**Where** two or three come together in my name, there I am with them."
Matthew 18:20

"Be **e(x)alted** O God, above the heavens; let your glory be over all the earth."
Psalm 57:5

"**You** are a chosen generation, a royal priesthood, a holy nation, a people belonging to God, that you may declare the praises of him who called you out of darkness into his marvelous light."
1 Peter 2:9

"**Zeal** for your house will consume me."
John 2:17

# A

*As* the deer pants for streams of water,
*so my soul pants for you O, God.*
Psalm 42:1

I have never been close enough to observe a deer panting. But my wife takes care of four outdoor cats, and I have seen them pant. Whenever Shelley sees this, she goes out and gives them a dish of fresh, cool water. They gladly lap it up and their panting ceases.

The author of this psalm obviously had seen deer so thirsty that they were panting. This must have made an impression on him. To see a wild animal in that state must have meant that, in that moment, the need for water was paramount. All other pursuits were unimportant by comparison.

The author of this psalm uses the analogy of this basic need to illustrate how predominant worship was to him. This image is an example of something significant for us as well. We were created to worship God, and we should make it a high priority in our lives.

**PRAYER:** Lord Jesus, You are the only source of "living water." May You put in my heart a thirst for worshipping You. May I look to You to provide the deepest needs of my soul.

# B

*__Be__ still and know that I am God.*
Psalm 46:10

In our fast-paced, busy world, this statement from the Lord could almost be considered a "hard saying." There are myriads of activities to choose from. Distractions abound. Just sitting still for a brief period can be difficult. Often our thoughts can run wild with all we have to or want to do.

Those of us with children know how challenging it can be to carve out quality time with them. An old saying goes, "How do you spell love to your children?" The answer: "T-I-M-E!" And while this saying may be an oversimplification, it does have a ring of truth.

If the Great Commandment is to love the Lord, how can we say we are doing that if we never sit still? We can truly show our love to God by giving Him our focused attention.

This verse may be relatively simple to memorize, but the real challenge is incorporating it into our daily lives.

**PRAYER:** Dear Lord, I so often take Your love for granted. Forgive me for my tendency to be distracted when what I truly desire is to be attentive. May my thoughts be less about my needs and more about quieting my heart and enjoying being in Your presence.

# C

*__Come__, let us sing for joy to the LORD;*
*let us shout to the Rock of our salvation.*
Psalm 95:1

During my ministry, music was always a huge emphasis for our worship service at Covenant of Grace. I led the singing of hymns, and my wife Shelley served as choir director and, later, full-time music director. We prioritized vibrant congregational singing. Even when we added a full praise band, we were sensitive that the music team did not overpower the singing of the worshippers.

One way we would occasionally accentuate congregational singing was for the piano to drop out so we could sing a cappella. Each year, one of the most moving moments of worship was on Christmas Eve. When we neared the end of the service, with the sanctuary lit only by soft candlelight, we would sing the third verse of Silent Night a cappella.

*Silent Night, holy night*
*Son of God, loves pure light*
*Radiant beams from thy holy face*
*with the dawn of redeeming grace*
*Jesus Lord at thy birth*
*Jesus Lord at thy birth*

To hear nothing but human voices was truly emotional and beautiful. God created us to sing praises to Him, and Psalm 95 reminds us to do just that.

~

**PRAYER:** Lord, what a joy and privilege it is to praise You in song. May I never tire of raising my voice in worship to You.

# D

*This is the **day** the LORD has made;*
*let us rejoice and be glad in it.*
Psalm 118:24

As a pastor, I have had the privilege of officiating about one hundred weddings. In the majority of these services, I have used this verse in my introductory remarks. For most people, their wedding day is one of the happiest times of their lives. It truly should be a wonderful experience of joy.

But a fair question to all believers is this: shouldn't this be the attitude we have every day? What if we not only memorized this verse but sought to live it daily? How different might things be if we allowed this verse to shape our attitude at the start of each day?

~

**PRAYER:** Heavenly Father, help me to remember each day that You grant me an opportunity to worship You. Instill in me the desire to make this verse the pattern of my life.

# E

*His love **endures** forever.*
Psalm 136:1

Psalm 136 is unique among the 150 psalms because of its distinctive antiphonal style. It was arranged for the leader to sing a statement of truth about God and then have the people reply with the refrain: *"His love endures forever."*

There is a certain irony in this verse being one of our 104 to memorize. The question that one may ask is, "Why is this refrain sung after each one of the twenty-six statements about God and His redemptive acts?" The reason for the repetition is obvious—so the people can memorize this invaluable truth about God's character.

In addition to the irony of this psalm, this verse gives me an opportunity to mention one of my favorite Hebrew words—*hesed*. While it is translated "love" in the NIV, the widely known King James Version translates it as "mercy." Many have memorized Psalm 23 in the King James with its last phrase, *"surely goodness and mercy shall follow me all the days of my life, and I will dwell in the house of the Lord forever."* The word mercy here is the Hebrew word *hesed*.

But a comprehensive study of the word reveals that it includes much more than the idea of mercy. Mercy is most often identified with favor that is underserved. But in its fullest sense, *hesed* not only describes God's compassion and kindness, but most of all, His covenant faithfulness to His children. *Hesed* may be best understood as the lovingkindness a parent has for their child. This is how we should understand God's love toward us.

**PRAYER:** Jesus, You taught your disciples to address God as our Heavenly Father. What a glorious truth. When I read Psalm 136, may I be reminded that this is the kind of love You have for me.

# F

*Let us **fix** our eyes on Jesus, the author*
*and perfecter of our faith.*
Hebrews 12:2

I do not like to admit it, but I have always struggled with being easily distracted. As a youth, in order to do my homework, I had to go to a room where no noise would affect my concentration. Even now, decades later, I must use this same discipline when I am writing or preparing a sermon.

One of the greatest things we can do to show our love for God in worship is to give Him our focused attention. In a world with so many distractions, this can be very challenging. When we love someone, one of the ways we can show that love is by being attentive. The same is true in our relationship with God.

This is one reason why worshipping God alongside other people is so important. When we come together to sing, pray, or listen to the proclamation of God's Word in a sermon, being with others of the same mindset helps us to keep our attention on one thing—worshipping God.

All of us are susceptible to being distracted. Remembering that, we can demonstrate our devotion to God by *"fixing our eyes on Jesus."*

**PRAYER:** Dear Lord, there are days when carving out time for daily devotion seems difficult. Even in church, my mind can drift as I think about events and duties I have later in the day. I acknowledge my struggle. By the power of Your Holy Spirit help me give You the focused attention You so richly deserve.

# G

*Ascribe to the L*ORD *the*
***glory*** *due his name.*
Psalm 29:2

Historic Presbyterians have the grand heritage of the work of the Westminster Assembly that wrote the Westminster Confession of Faith and the Larger and Shorter Catechisms. According to the famous church historian Phillip Schaff, these were the concluding documents of the period known as the Protestant Reformation.

Perhaps the most well-known part of all that effort is the wording of Question #1 of the Shorter Catechism which asks: "What is the chief end of man?"

The answer is so memorable because it is both short and profound: "To glorify God and enjoy Him forever."

We cannot add to God's glory. He is glorious beyond any limit. But we were created to declare and magnify that glory by giving God worship.

The Old Testament word for glory is the word *kabod*, which

has the idea of "one being laden with riches." The New Testament word *doxa* has the connotation of "giving recognition of honor and acclaim."

God is laden with riches beyond description and as such deserves recognition for who He is and what He has done. To give "God the glory due His name" is both the believer's great privilege and responsibility.

**PRAYER:** Almighty and Everlasting God, my words can never adequately give You the glory You deserve. But I am so thankful that You have enabled me to glorify You by becoming more like Your Son.

# H

*__How__ great is the love the Father has
lavished on us, that we should be called
children of God! And that is what we are.*
1 John 3:1

It is interesting that followers of Jesus were not referred to as Christians until they received that label in Antioch, Syria, in Acts 11:26.

While this name became the widely accepted term, in the third chapter of his letter to the churches, John makes it very clear that God calls us "children." To be a beloved child of God is one of the most precious ways to describe a believer in Jesus. John stresses how much God loves us. God "lavishes" His children with love. And after John says that once, he makes it emphatic by saying, "And that is what we are!"

A contemporary Christian song that I love is, *I Am Who You Say I Am*. Throughout the song, it repeats the main thought of 1 John 3:1, with the refrain, "I'm a child of God. Yes I am!"

Along with preaching the Gospel to ourselves every day, it would behoove us to recite or even sing this song as a declaration of God's great love for us and cherish the privilege we have as children of God.

**PRAYER:** Father, thank You for choosing me to become Your child. Thank You for all the wonderful privileges that are mine because, through faith in Jesus, I am adopted into Your family.

# I

*If we confess our sins, he is faithful
and just and will forgive us our sins
and purify us from all unrighteousness.*
1 John 1:9

In four decades of preparing corporate worship services, I may have used this verse more often than any other. When we place our trust in Jesus Christ as our Savior, justification occurs. All our sins —past, present, and future—are paid for by Christ's finished work on the cross. Because Jesus dwells within us by His Spirit, God sees us as completely righteous.

But on an experiential level, we still are capable of sinning. In fact, we do continue to sin. That will be our constant struggle until we are glorified when we get to heaven.

Jesus explained our need for daily cleansing in His conversation with Peter in the Upper Room just before the Last Supper (John 13:4–10). When Jesus went to wash Peter's feet, Peter objected. After Jesus explained to him why it was necessary to do this, Peter asked Jesus to wash him all over.

Jesus' answer is an illustration of the meaning of today's memory verse. He tells Peter: *"A person who has had a bath needs only to wash his feet, his whole body is clean"* (1 John 13:10).

Once we profess Christ as our Savior and repent of our sins, we are forgiven eternally. But when we sin in our daily walk on this earth, asking for forgiveness is similar to the feeling of being cleansed that occurred with foot-washing in Jesus' day. That cleansing enables us to enjoy fellowship with Jesus in a renewed way.

**PRAYER:** Father, through faith in Your Son, I know my sins are forgiven. Help me be aware of the times that I do not please You and go against Your will. May I be quick to confess those things and experience the cleansing that You promise.

# J

*Through **Jesus**, therefore, let us continually*
*offer to God a sacrifice of praise—*
*the fruit of lips that confess his name.*
Hebrews 13:15

One of the main themes of the Book of Hebrews is the "supremacy of Christ." In today's verse, we see the need for Christ to be specifically connected with the worship of God. This should seem obvious for all Christian worshippers.

Is it possible to effectively worship God and yet keep the name or thought of Jesus completely out of the activity? The answer is, "No."

Bryan Chapell has written an excellent book that has a very catchy title that may give us insight into this verse. His book on prayer is entitled *Praying Backwards*. The book's main idea is that we should remember the significance of Jesus even as we begin our prayer.

The most frequently used ending of Christian prayer is the

phrase, "in Jesus' name." The appropriateness of praying like this is that it reflects the very significant truth that our prayers are heard by our Heavenly Father because of the merit and mediation of God's Son, Jesus Christ. (1 Timothy 2:5) We would do well to remember that, as we begin our prayer, our prayers are heard because of the mediatorial work of Jesus.

**PRAYER:** Father, may I always remember that without You sending Your Son, all my efforts to bring You worship would be in vain. As I come before You in worship and in prayer, may I remember to include Jesus and His sacrifice on the cross in my thoughts.

# K

*Your __kingdom__ is an everlasting kingdom, and*
*your dominion endures through all generations.*
Psalm 145:13

One of the ways I seek to honor the 5th Commandment by resting on the Sabbath is to avoid looking at news on my phone or TV. Being bombarded by the evil and calamity in the world can be stressful, not restful.

That is why we need to daily feed on God's Word. Reading verses from Scripture like this reminds us that we are living in God's kingdom. It is His dominion, He is Lord, and one day, evil will be no more, and righteousness will prevail in all areas of life.

To be a member of God's kingdom is to know that someday His rule will come to earth. There will be a new heaven and new earth. We can give God worship and praise every day in anticipation that that day will come.

**PRAYER:** Jesus, You taught your disciples to pray, *"Thy kingdom come, thy will be done, on earth as it is in heaven."* May I see myself as an ambassador of Your kingdom. Help me to remember when I get discouraged, that one day, as You have promised, all wrongs will be made right, and You will permanently dwell on earth with Your people.

# L

*The **Lord** is gracious and compassionate,*
*slow to anger and rich in love.*
Psalm 145:8

Psalm 145 is one of my favorite psalms. You will find more descriptions of the character of God in this psalm than in any other chapter in the Bible. Verse after verse, we read why we should give praise and worship to Him.

Obviously, there are many traits describing God's character. But none appear linked together as often as the four traits we find here in Psalm 145:8. Between Exodus 34:6 and Psalm 145, there are five other times when this combination of four traits is grouped together in one verse.

The greatest proof of this truth is God's sending His Son to take on human flesh, to die for our sins and be raised from the dead. These four qualities are where we should start when we think about the character of God. They all are demonstrated for us in the person and work of our Savior, Jesus Christ.

**PRAYER:** Father, so often my prayers seem like a grocery list as I bring my needs before You. Help me develop in my prayer life the pattern of remembering You—just for who You are. Let me never forget that You are *"gracious and compassionate, slow to anger and rich in love."*

# M

*God is spirit, and his worshippers*
**<u>must</u>** *worship in spirit and in truth.*
John 4:24

I have a dear friend who is an amazing musician. In addition to being an outstanding orchestra conductor, he was the paid organist of a very large church for a time. He once told me how difficult it was to worship God while being responsible for all the music in the service. I suppose that is a struggle for all musicians who are worship leaders.

As a pastor who was responsible for planning worship services throughout my career, I also led the singing of hymns and rotated as a guitarist and vocalist on the worship team. One of the things I did to minimize distractions was to go through the words of the music on Saturday night. This would allow me to focus and not worry about making a mistake either in the order of the service or in the music.

Also, when I was on the worship team, in our prayer following our warm-up, I would frequently pray that as musicians, we would be able to personally worship God as we lead worship. Leaders can get caught up in leading and forget that all the glory should go to Jesus. Worshipping in spirit is just worshipping sincerely from the heart.

Worshipping in truth is also a must. It means worshipping God according to His revealed character. The Bible is our guide in this area and gives us all we need to know.

**PRAYER:** Father, may this verse remind me that I must worship in the same way I am to love You—with my whole being—heart, soul, mind, and strength.

# N

*Let us **not** give up meeting together,*
*as some are in the habit of doing.*
Hebrews 10:25

The COVID-19 pandemic was difficult for everyone. It was hard on our congregation. Not only did the disease create great fear and resulted in many deaths, we also had to wear masks and withdraw from people. For months, our church was closed by order of the governor, and our worship was confined to my preaching a Sunday-morning sermon on my cellphone that was then uploaded onto social media platforms.

Once there were vaccines and the risk of serious consequences from the virus became less of a threat, we reopened our doors to worship in person. And, although the virtual worship experience added a new opportunity for shut-ins and for people who were temporarily not feeling well, for others it became the norm to worship virtually instead of attending in person.

The writer of Hebrews was speaking to a group of professing

Christians who were neglecting corporate worship as well. Although their reason for not gathering obviously was fear of persecution, Hebrews 10:25 warns Christians of all generations, in all circumstances, that without good reason, we will miss a great blessing if we abandon worshipping with other believers.

**PRAYER:** Lord God, You are worthy of my worship. Out of love for You and the need of my own heart, may I be faithful in making the practice of worshipping with other believers a valuable part of my life.

# O

*O LORD, our Lord, how majestic*
*is your name in all the earth.*
Psalm 8:1

In her poem *America the Beautiful*, author Katherine Bates, attempts to paint with words the splendor of our country. The song begins, "O, beautiful for spacious skies, for amber waves of grain." Then it continues with the words, "for purple mountains majesty above the fruited plain." Mountain peaks are frequently used to portray majesty because they stand above and seem superior to anything around them.

In Psalm 8:1, God is described as majestic. There is nothing that can compare to Him. Like a magnificent mountain that rises above its surroundings, God's greatness and splendor are unsurpassed. And even as a mountain seems to overlook all that is around it, so too, God is above all that He has created.

I love the outdoors, whether it be a rippling brook, ocean waves crashing against a beach, or a sunset with its impressive array of colors. The earth and all its splendor reflect our great God who brought it into being.

**PRAYER:** O God, whenever I take in the beauty of the natural world that surrounds us, may I remember that You are the Creator of it all and give You praise.

# P

*__Praise__ be to the God and Father*
*of our Lord Jesus Christ!*
1 Peter 1:3

Ten years ago, a lump was detected at my wife Shelley's annual mammogram. After the procedure was completed, the technician gave her a worried look and said, "You need to follow up with your doctor immediately." Her doctor ordered a biopsy of the tissue, and on Thanksgiving Day, my wife received a short and rather terse phone call from the same doctor saying it was cancerous but of a type that should not spread.

Following a total mastectomy at the Breast Center at Johns Hopkins Hospital, we were told that the cancer had indeed spread into the lymph system, and it was recommended that she receive radiation treatments. After forty consecutive treatments, a PET Scan was prescribed to see if the cancer had spread to any major organs. We were told to wait after the scan and receive the results from the radiologist.

When the doctor came out and told us that the PET scan was clear, with tears in my eyes, I wrapped my arms around my wife and cried out, "Praise the Lord!" What my wife noticed was how the three women in the office all began to tear up as they also felt my joy that my precious wife was cancer-free.

Praise may be best described as homage rendered to God in worship of His person and thanksgiving for His favors and blessings. Praise can be expressed in private and, as in my example, in public. We were created to give God praise and the reasons and occasions have no bounds.

**PRAYER:** Father, we were designed to give You praise because we were created to worship You. May my days be filled with praise for all that You are and all that You do.

# Q

*Come with me by yourselves to a*
**quiet** *place and get some rest.*
Mark 6:31

There are many who see the ultimate Christian life as keeping very busy in service and running from one ministry opportunity to another.

There is no question that God has called us to serve as a way of showing His love. But here in Mark 6, Jesus calls His disciples to slow down and rest by spending quality time alone with Him.

"Quiet Time" is a well-known Christian term for private devotions. In our American, fast-paced culture, it is easy to neglect this vital part of our spiritual life. Jesus modeled this and asked the same of His disciples. Spending time alone with Jesus, learning, listening, and reflecting on His words is a spiritual habit we should not neglect regardless of the many activities that occupy our time.

**PRAYER:** Thank You, Jesus, for reminding me to set apart alone time with You. May this verse teach me that in Your earthly ministry, You told Your disciples to spend quiet time alone with You and rest. Help me make this a regular part of my life.

# R

*What do you have that*
*you did not **receive**?*
1 Corinthians 4:7

I discovered this verse fairly late in my pastoral ministry. But I am so glad I found it, for the word "receive" brings to mind the idea of a gift. This verse points out how we should view the blessings that come our way.

When we receive a gift, we should be thankful. Thankfulness is one of the basic elements of worship. With hard work and constant practice, we can develop our talents and opportunities, but God is ultimately responsible for what we have. When we fail to give God credit, we are being short-sighted.

Hopefully we realize that all of our abilities and opportunities are in some way the result of God's sovereign will. Because of this truth, let us give Him praise and thanks. As James put it so well in his letter to the churches: *"Every good and perfect gift is from above, coming down from the Father of heavenly lights"* (James 1:17).

**PRAYER:** Father, I am often quick to give myself credit for my successes. Forgive me for my short-sightedness. Please help me to remember that Your gracious hand is behind all the good things that come to me.

# S

*__Sing__ to the Lord a new song.*
Psalm 96:1

I love the great old hymns of the church. I heard Cliff Barrow, Billy Graham's song leader for his evangelistic crusades, once say: "We don't sing the great old hymns because they're old. We sing them because they are great." Singing the "great old hymns" of the church keeps us connected to our Christian heritage of the past.

But we should not be limited to just singing our favorite old hymns and songs. Although something new may be uncomfortable at times, singing new songs to God is consistent with what Psalm 96:1 tells us to do.

It also reminds us that God is a creative God. We can express our God-given creativity by writing new songs or new arrangements to established tunes and lyrics. Then sing them.

Singing is an important way of expressing praise in worship. Let us sing our new songs so that, in a fresh way, others can hear who God is or what He has done in our lives.

**PRAYER:** Lord, there are certain styles of worship music that I prefer. May You expand my horizons in appreciating Christian music that is different from my preferred taste. And in doing so may I grow in my worship of You.

T

*__This__ is love: not that we loved God,
but that he loved us and sent his Son as
an atoning sacrifice for our sins.*
1 John 4:10

When I was in my teens, the Beatles were at the height of their popularity. Although I loved their music, at the time I was not very discerning about the messages in their songs. One such single was, "All You Need Is Love." It sounded appealing to so many in my generation and still has much of the same effect today.

But the song begs the question: "What is love?" If that is all you need, it should be all-encompassing. Unfortunately, the Beatle's song merely romanticizes love, and we are left with no clear substance or meaning of what love actually is.

While love—properly defined—should include many aspects, the Bible, and this verse in particular, makes the concept of sacrifice a key part of real love. God's love is demonstrated in sacrificial action, not in fuzzy feelings.

Jesus hung on the cross to take our sins upon Himself so we could be forgiven, redeemed, and brought into the family of God. Love is demonstrated through action, not mere emotion. So, when we think of a definition of love, the word "sacrifice" should be included.

**PRAYER:** Father, when things seem difficult or not going the way I want at times, I may doubt that You love me. In those moments, may You bring this verse to mind and help me remember that sending Your Son to die on the cross for my sin is the undeniable proof of Your love.

# U

*Have mercy on me, O God,*
*according to your **unfailing** love.*
Psalm 51:1

One of my favorite responsibilities as a pastor was officiating weddings. Unless there were extraordinary circumstances, I required the couple to attend six pre-marital counseling sessions.

One session focused on effective communication. I noted from counseling troubled marriages in the past, that couples generally did not know how to ask for forgiveness, and I shared with them a clear, biblical process.

Ephesians 4:32 states the main reason why Christians can forgive one another. Paul instructs the churches in Ephesus, *"Be kind and compassionate to one another, forgiving each other, just as God in Christ forgave you."*

But nowhere in the Bible is forgiveness explained as well as David's Psalm 51. At the core of David's request is his deep and abiding understanding of the character of God. He has the audacity to ask God to forgive him despite his adultery and treachery because he truly believes that God is compassionate and gracious.

But he also knows that God is holy, so David understands that close fellowship with the Lord is not possible until forgiveness has been sincerely requested. Because he knows that God is compassionate, David is certain he will receive forgiveness.

**PRAYER:** Father, I am an unworthy sinner deserving only Your displeasure and righteous judgment. But through the work of Jesus Christ on my behalf, I know You are a God of mercy and unfailing love.

# V

*Therefore, I urge you, brothers, in **view** of God's mercy, to offer your bodies as living sacrifices.*
Romans 12:1

I loved and deeply respected my father-in-law, George Armacost. He may not have finished the ninth grade, but he was an outstanding farmer, a tireless truck driver, and an excellent mechanic. He could fix just about anything.

But what was so special about George was his servant's heart. If anyone was in need, he would drop whatever he was doing and lend a hand. When he died suddenly at age eighty, over five hundred people came to his viewing to pay their respects. I believe it was because of the unselfish servant's heart he had demonstrated over the years.

My brother-in-law, Mike, had witnessed this quality countless times. Right before I officiated the funeral, with tears in his eyes, he told me, "George was the most Christ-like man I ever knew."

Throughout this book, I have stated that we are saved by faith and not by works. But our verse for today links service to others as a genuine way we can glorify God. A quote from the famous theologian Martin Luther may give us some valuable insight, "We are saved by faith alone. But the faith that saves is not alone."

**PRAYER**: Lord, help me to understand from this verse that my worship of You is not limited to Sunday morning services or my individual quiet times. Help me to see that I can worship You through service to others as well.

# W

*Where two or three come together*
*in my name, there I am with them.*
Matthew 18:20

Everyone in America born before 1990 can probably remember where they were on September 11, 2001. My wife and I received a call that morning regarding the initial attack on one of the Twin Towers and turned on the TV. To our great horror, we watched the second tower crumble to the ground.

We were shocked and stunned! At that moment, we had no idea how the world would change as a result of this evil event.

Realizing that the members of our congregation would also be feeling anxious and distressed, we decided to have a special prayer meeting at Covenant of Grace that evening. We sent the word out on our prayer chain communication. That night about 3/4th of our congregation came out to ask for God's comfort and assurance that He was in control, despite what seemed to be a senseless, heinous attack on our country. We also prayed for our leaders to know how to respond appropriately to what had just happened.

In Matthew 18:20, Jesus promises to be with His people in a significant way when they gather as a group "in His name." I believe the application includes times of worship, times of special celebration, and also traumatic circumstances when His presence is especially needed and desired.

**PRAYER:** Jesus, knowing that You promise to be with us when we gather is a great comfort. Help me not to neglect or shy away from opportunities that arise where I can experience Your presence when gathering with other believers.

# X

*Be **e(x)alted**, O God, above the heavens;*
*let your glory be over all the earth.*
Psalm 57:5

Our middle son, Bradley, was an outstanding high school basketball player. As a senior, he was 6'5" and the starting center of the team. Years later at a Ravens game, as he was looking for the gate where his seat was located, Bradley noticed the Washington Bullets NBA player George Muresan. Muresan was 7'7" and had the distinction of being the tallest person to ever play basketball in the NBA.

Seeing a unique opportunity, Bradley walked up to Muresan and asked if he could have his picture taken with him. In a very gruff voice, Muresan replied, "Why?"

Undeterred, my son answered, "My wife thinks I am so tall. She thinks it would be really cool if I got a picture with someone so much taller than me." With that explanation, Muresan agreed, and Bradley got his photo with this giant of a man.

In its ancient literal meaning, the word "exalted" had to do with being very high or superior in physical position. In practical usage, the word takes on the meaning of that which is elevated in rank, influence, character, or power. The proper way to worship God is to view Him as above or superior to everything in every way.

Picturing the heavens is probably the highest thing that we can imagine. Yet Psalm 57:5 tells us that God surpasses even that: *"Be exalted, O God, above the heavens, let your glory be over all of the earth."* Only God is above the heavens. So in our worship, we should constantly be thinking about ways we can express His greatness.

**PRAYER:** Our exalted and gracious God, there are times when I want to bring You down to my level. When I hear the word "exalted" spoken or sung, may it cause me to think about Your greatness and desire to give You the highest praise.

# Y

*<u>**You**</u> are a chosen generation, a royal priesthood,*
*a holy nation, a people belonging to God, that you*
*may declare the praises of him who called you*
*out of darkness into his wonderful light.*
1 Peter 2:9

For the majority of the years I pastored, we used Scripture choruses as a regular part of our worship service. One of the things I loved about those choruses was that they often were just verses straight out of the Bible.

1 Peter 2:9 was one of my favorites. Not only did it have an upbeat tempo, but it also had two very meaningful messages.

First, it describes how God views us in Christ. We are chosen of God. We are princes and princesses because we are children of the King. We are priests and are given the sacred responsibility to intercede for people. We are holy because Christ is in us. We are a national entity. And we are God's cherished possession.

That is how God sees us.

But this verse not only tells us how valued we are in God's sight; it also states that we have a vital role in advancing His kingdom. We are called by God to tell others that through faith in Christ, we have been freed from the darkness of sin and have been brought into the very light of His presence.

**PRAYER:** Father thank You for my privileged status. May I seek to live up to who You say I am and what You have called me to do.

# Z

*__Zeal__ for your house will consume me.*
John 2:17

"Zeal" is an emotional word, and "intense passion" is very close to its meaning. John 2:17 is a significant example of how passionate Jesus was about right worship.

In John 2, the disciples recall this verse from the Old Testament after seeing Jesus tip over the tables of the moneychangers. He also drives out those who are making exorbitant profits from selling animals for sacrifice. We are told that Jesus says to these scoundrels, "How dare you turn my Father's house into a market!"

So how can memorizing this verse benefit our lives? It shows how fervent Jesus was in defending the honor of His Father's house and how important and sacred worship was to Him.

As we come to our very last memory verse, may it remind us to have zeal in our worship of God as well.

**PRAYER:** Jesus, when I remember when You cleansed the Temple, may it remind me of how zealous You were to honor Your Father's house and to protect the integrity of true worship.

# Appendix A
## Verses Grouped by First Letter of the Key Word

**A**

"**All** Scripture is God-breathed and is useful for teaching, rebuking, correcting and training in righteousness."
2 Timothy 3:16

"**Ask** and it shall be given to you; seek and you will find; knock and the door will be opened to you."
Matthew 7:7

"**All** have sinned and fall short of the glory of God."
Romans 3:23

"**As** the deer pants for streams of water, so my soul pants for you, O God."
Psalm 42:1

**B**

"**But** grow in the grace and knowledge of our Lord and Savior Jesus Christ."
2 Peter 3:18

"**But** those who hope in the LORD will renew their strength. They will soar on wings like eagles; they will run and not grow weary, they will walk and not be faint."
Isaiah 40:31

"**Be** perfect, therefore, as your heavenly Father is perfect."
Matthew 5:48

"**Be** still, and know that I am God."
Psalm 46:10

## C

"**Cast** all your anxiety on him because he cares for you."
1 Peter 5:7

"**Consider** it pure joy my brothers when you face trials of many kinds, because you know the testing of your faith develops perseverance."
James 1:2

"**Come** to me, all who are weary and burdened, and I will give you rest."
Matthew 11:28

"**Come,** let us sing for joy to the LORD; let us shout to the Rock of our salvation."
Psalm 95:1

## D

"**Delight** yourself in the Lord and he will give you the desires of your heart."
Psalm 37:4

"**Do** not fear, for I have redeemed you; I have called you by name: you are Mine!"
Isaiah 43:1

"You believe that there is only one God. Good! Even the **demons** believe that and shudder."
James 2:19

"This is the **day** the LORD has made. Let us rejoice and be glad in it."
Psalm 118:34

**E**
"**Encourage** one another daily, as long as it called Today."
Hebrews 3:13

"I lift up my **eyes** to the hills—where does my help come from? My help comes from the LORD, the Maker of heaven and earth."
Psalm 121:1-2

"The gift of God is **eternal** life in Christ Jesus our Lord."
Romans 6:23

"His love **endures** forever."
Psalm 136:1

**F**
"**For** I know the plans I have for you, declares the LORD, plans to prosper you and not to harm you, plans to give you hope and a future."
Jeremiah 29:11

"**Faith** comes from hearing the message, and the message is heard through the word of Christ."
Romans 10:17

"**For** it is by grace you have been saved through faith, and this not from yourselves, it is the gift of God—not by works, so that no one can boast."
Ephesians 2:8-9

"Let us **fix** our eyes on Jesus, the author and perfecter of our faith."
Hebrews 12:2

**G**
"**God** is our refuge and strength, an ever-present help in trouble."
Psalm 46:1

"**God** demonstrates his own love for us in this: While we were still sinners Christ died for us."
Romans 5:8

"**God** so loved the world that he gave his one and only Son, that whoever believes in him shall not perish but have eternal life."
John 3:16

"Ascribe to the LORD the **glory** due his name."
Psalm 29:2

**H**
"**He** himself is our peace."
Ephesians 2:14

"In **him** and through faith in him we may approach God with freedom and confidence."
Ephesians 3:12

"**He** himself bore our sins in his body on the tree, that we might die to sins and live for righteousness; by his wounds you have been healed."
1 Peter 2:24

"**How** great the love the Father has lavished on us, that we should be called children of God. And that is what we are."
1 John 3:1

I
"**I** tell you the truth, he who believes has eternal life."
John 6:47

"**I** can do all things through Christ who strengthens me."
Philippians 4:13 NKJV

"**It** is finished."
John 19:20

"**If** we confess our sins, he is faithful and just and will forgive us our sins and purify us from all unrighteousness."
1 John 1:9

J
"The **joy** of the LORD is your strength."
Nehemiah 8:10

"**Join** me in my struggle by praying to God for me."
Romans 15:30

"**Jesus** answered, 'The work of God is this: to believe in the one he has sent'."
John 6:29

"Through **Jesus,** therefore, let us continually offer to God a sacrifice of praise—the fruit of lips that praise his name."
Hebrews 13:15

## K

"And we **know** that in all things God works for the good of those who love him, who have been called according to his purpose."
Romans 8:28

"**Know** that the LORD, he is God; It is he who has made us and not we ourselves."
Psalm 100:3 NKJV

"All men will **know** that you are my disciples if you love one another."
John 13:35

"Your **kingdom** is an everlasting kingdom, and your dominion endures through all generations."
Psalm 145:13

## L

"**Love** the Lord your God with all your heart and with all your soul and with all your mind and with all your strength."
Mark 12:30

"**Live** by faith, not by sight."
2 Corinthians 5:7

"God is **love**."
1 John 4:16

"The **LORD** is gracious and compassionate, slow to anger
and rich in love."
Psalm 145:8

# M

"**My** grace is sufficient for you, for my power is made
perfect in weakness."
1 Corinthians 12:9

"**My** soul finds rest in God alone; my salvation comes from
him."
Psalm 62:1

"Thomas said to him, '**My** Lord and my God!'"
John 20: 28

"God is spirit, and his worshippers **must** worship in spirit
and in truth."
John 4:24

# N

"**Now** that you know these things, you will be blessed if
you do them."
John 13:19

"**Now** faith is the assurance of things hoped for, the
conviction of things not seen."
Hebrews 11:1 NASB

"**Now** this is eternal life: that they may know you, the only true God, and Jesus Christ. whom you have sent."
John 17:3

"Let us **not** give up meeting together, as some are in the habit of doing."
Hebrews 10:25

## O

"To **obey** is better than sacrifice."
1 Samuel 15:22

"The **only** thing that counts is faith expressing itself through love."
Galatians 5:6

"Believe **on** the Lord Jesus Christ, and you will be saved."
Acts 16:31 NKJV

"**O** LORD, our Lord, how majestic is your name in all the earth!"
Psalm 8:1

## P

"The **plans** of the LORD stand forever, the purposes of his heart through all generations."
Psalm 33:11

"**Pray** continually."
1 Thessalonians 5:17

"I am not ashamed of the gospel, because it is the **power** of God for the salvation of everyone who believes."
Romans 1:9

"**Praise** be to the God and Father of our Lord Jesus Christ!"
1 Peter 1:4

# Q

"Everyone should be **quick** to listen, slow to speak, and slow to become angry."
James 1:19

"You **quarrel** and fight. You do not have, because you do not ask God."
James 4:2

"For since the creation of the world God's invisible **qualities**—his eternal power and divine nature—have been clearly seen, being understood from what has been made, so that men are without excuse."
Romans 1:20

"Come to me by yourselves to a **quiet** place and get some rest."
Mark 6:31

# R

"**Rejoice** in the Lord always. I will say it again: Rejoice! Let your gentleness be evident to all. The Lord is near."
Philippians 4:4

"The **righteous** will live by faith."
Romans 1:17

"For as far as the east is from the west, so far has he **removed** our transgressions from us."
Psalm 103:12

"What do you have that you did not **receive**?"
1 Corinthians 4:7

**S**
"**Seek** first his kingdom and his righteousness, and all these things will be given to you as well."
Matthew 6:33

"David found **strength** in the LORD his God."
1 Samuel 30:6

"If you confess with your mouth, 'Jesus is Lord', and believe in your heart God raised him from the dead, you will be **saved**."
Romans 10:9

"**Sing** to the LORD a new song."
Psalm 96:1

**T**
"**Therefore**, go and make disciples of all nations, baptizing them in the name of the Father and of the Son and of the Holy Spirit, and teaching them to obey all I have commanded you."
Matthew 28:19–20

"**Trust** in the LORD with all your heart and lean not on your own understanding: in all your ways acknowledge him, and he will make your paths straight."
Proverbs 3:5–6

"I write these **things** to you who believe in the name of the Son of God, so that that you may know that you have eternal life."
John 5:13

"**This** is love: not that we loved God, but that he loved us and sent his Son as an atoning sacrifice for our sins."
1 John 4:10

## U

"**Unless** the LORD builds the house, its builders labor in vain."
Psalm 127:1

"I do believe. Help me overcome my **unbelief**!"
Mark 9:24

"The Word became flesh and lived for a while among **us**."
John 1:14

"Have mercy on me O God, according to your **unfailing** love."
Psalm 51:1

## V

"This is the **verdict**: light has come into the world."
John 3:19

"This is the **victory** that has overcome the world, even our faith."
1 John 5:4

"I stand at the door and knock. If anyone hears my **voice** and opens the door, I will go in and eat with him, and he with me."
Revelation 3:20

"Therefore, I urge you, brothers, in **view** of God's mercy, to offer your bodies as living sacrifices."
Romans 12:1

**W**
"**Work** out your salvation with fear and trembling for it is God who works in you to will and to act according to his good purpose."
Philippians 2:12–13

"**Without** faith, it is impossible to please God, for anyone who comes to him must believe he exists and rewards those who earnestly seek him."
Hebrews 11:6

"**We** all, like sheep, have gone astray, each of us has turned to his own way; and the LORD has laid on him the iniquity of us all."
Isaiah 53:6

"**Where** two or three come together in my name, there I am with them."
Matthew 18:20

**X**
"Righteousness **e(x)alts** a nation, but sin is a disgrace to any people."
Proverbs 14:34

"**E(x)cel** in everything, in faith, in speech, in knowledge, in complete earnestness and in your love."
2 Corinthians 8:7

"Set an **e(x)ample** for the believers in speech, in life, in love, in faith and in purity."
1 Timothy 4:12

"Be **e(x)alted,** O God, above the heavens; let your glory be over all the earth." Psalm 57:5

**Y**
"**You** will seek me and find me when you seek me with all your heart."
Jeremiah 29:13

"**Yea**, though I walk through the valley of the shadow of death I will fear no evil, for You are with me."
Psalm 23:4 NKJV

"**Yet** to all who received him, to those who believed in his name, to them he gave the right to be called children of God."
John 1:12

"**You** are a chosen generation, a royal priesthood, a holy nation, a people belonging to God, that you may declare the praises of him who called you out of darkness into his wonderful light."
1 Peter 2:9-10

**Z**
"It is not good to have **zeal** without knowledge."
Proverbs 19:2

"The **zeal** of the LORD Almighty will accomplish this."
Isaiah 9:7

"Never be lacking in **zeal**, but keep your spiritual fervor,
serving the Lord."
Romans 12:11

"**Zeal** for your house will consume me."
John 2:1

# APPENDIX B
## TIPS FOR MEMORIZING SCRIPTURE

1. Make a commitment to the task.
2. Admit to yourself that it will take much work and practice.
3. Set a realistic goal for yourself.
4. Pray for God's help in memorizing these verses.
5. Decide on which of the four categories you wish to memorize first and stick to that group.
6. Decide how many verses you want to memorize each week.
7. Write the verse out at least ten times; then write it out by memory.
8. When you write the verse, say it out loud.
9. Write a flash card for each verse.
10. Record the verse(s) and play it in the car while driving.
11. Try and recite the verses out loud as you commute to work or on your way home.
12. Seek to apply the verse in your life. Offer a sincere prayer to God that He would help you live out this verse.

13. Recite the verse or verses you have memorized out loud.

14. Say the verse(s) to yourself just before going to sleep at night.

15. Keep reviewing and practicing the verses in alphabetical order. Let the key word help you remember the rest of the words in the verse.

16. Include memorizing the verse reference.

17. Photocopy Appendix C and use it to quiz yourself by writing in the words and then checking to see if you are correct.

18. Review the verses you have previously memorized on a regular basis.

19. If you have a different verse you want to memorize, write it into the book and find a key word that works alphabetically

20. Memorize with a friend.

# APPENDIX C
## QUIZZES

## ENCOURAGEMENT MEMORY VERSES SELF-QUIZ

**All** _____ __ God- breathed ___ __ _____ __

_____, _____, _____ ___ _____ __

_____.

2 Timothy 2:16

**But** grow __ ____ _____ ___knowledge __ ___ ____ ____

_____ .

2 Peter 3:18

**Cast** ___ ____ anxiety__ ____ _____ __ cares ___ ___.

1 Peter 5:7

**Delight** _____ __ ___ ____ ___ __ ____ give ____ ___

desires __ ____ _____.

Psalm 37:4

**Encourage** ___ _____ daily, __ ____ __ __ __ ____ today.

Hebrews 3:13

**For** _ ____ ___ plans _ ____ ___ ___ , _____ ___ ___ .
____ __ prosper ___ ___ ___ _ ___ ___ , ____ __ ___ ___
hope ___ _ _____ .
*Jeremiah 29:11*

**God** __ ___ *refuge* ___ _____ , _ ___ _____ *help* __
_____ .
Psalm 46:1

**He** _____ __ ___ peace.
Ephesians 2:14

**I** ___ ___ ___ ____ , __ ___ believes ___ _____ ___ .
John 6:47

The **joy** __ ___ ____ __ your _____ .
Nehemiah 8:10

And __ **know** ____ ___ ___ _____ ___ works ___ ___ good __
_____ ___ ___ ___ , ___ ___ ___ called _____ ___ ___
_____ .
Romans 8:28

**Love** ___ ___ ____ ___ ____ ___ __ heart ___ ___ ___
____ soul ___ ___ ___ ____ mind ___ ___ ___ ___
_____ .
Mark 12:30

**My** _____ __ sufficient ___ ___ , ___ __ power __ ____ perfect
__ _____ .
2 Corinthians 12:9

**Now** \_\_\_\_ \_\_ know \_\_\_\_\_ _____ , \_\_\_ \_\_\_\_ \_\_ blessed \_\_
\_\_\_ do \_\_\_\_.
John 13:17

To **obey** \_\_ _____ \_\_\_\_ sacrifice.
1 Samuel 15:22

The **plans** \_\_ \_\_\_ \_\_\_\_ \_\_\_\_ forever, \_\_\_ _____ \_\_ \_\_
\_\_\_\_ through \_\_\_ _____ .
Psalm 33:11

Everyone _____ \_\_ **quick** \_\_ listen, \_\_\_\_\_ \_\_ \_\_\_\_\_ , \_\_\_ \_\_\_\_
\_\_ become \_\_\_\_\_ .
James 1:19

**Rejoice** \_\_ \_\_\_ \_\_\_\_ always. \_ \_\_\_\_ \_\_\_ \_\_\_ again : \_\_\_\_\_ ! \_\_\_
\_\_\_\_ _____ \_\_ _____ \_\_ \_\_\_. \_\_\_ \_\_\_\_ \_\_ \_\_\_\_ .
Philippians 4:4

**Seek** \_\_\_\_\_ \_\_ kingdom \_\_\_ \_\_\_ _____ , \_\_\_ \_\_
\_\_\_\_\_ \_\_\_\_\_ \_\_\_\_ \_\_ given \_\_ \_\_\_ \_\_ \_\_\_\_ .
Matthew 6:33

**Therefore**, \_\_ \_\_\_ \_\_\_\_\_ disciples \_\_ \_\_\_ nations , _____
\_\_\_\_ \_\_ \_\_ \_\_\_\_ \_\_ \_\_\_ Father \_\_\_ \_\_ \_\_\_ \_\_\_\_ \_\_\_ \_\_\_\_
\_\_\_\_ \_\_\_\_\_ .
Matthew 28:19–20

**Unless** \_\_\_ \_\_\_\_\_ builds \_\_\_ \_\_\_\_\_ , \_\_\_ _____ labor \_\_
\_\_\_\_ .
Psalm 127:1

**This** \_\_ \_\_\_ **verdict:** Light\_\_\_ \_\_\_\_ \_\_\_\_ \_\_\_ *world*.
John 3:19

**Work** \_\_\_ \_\_\_ *salvation* \_\_\_\_ *fear* \_\_\_ _____ , \_\_\_ \_\_ \_\_ \_\_
\_\_ \_\_\_\_ \_\_ *you* \_\_ \_\_\_\_ \_\_\_ \_\_ \_\_\_ *accordingly* \_\_ \_\_\_ \_\_\_
_____ .
Philippians 2:12

Righteousness **e(x)alts** \_ _____ , \_\_\_ \_\_\_ \_\_ \_ disgrace \_\_ any
\_\_\_\_\_ .
Proverbs 14:34

**You** \_\_\_ seek \_\_ \_\_\_ find \_\_ \_\_\_\_ \_\_\_ \_\_\_\_ \_\_ \_\_\_\_ \_\_\_ \_\_\_\_
heart.
Jeremiah 29:13

It \_\_ not good \_\_ \_\_\_\_ **zeal** without _____ .
Proverbs 19:2

## FAITH MEMORY VERSES SELF-QUIZ

**Ask** \_\_\_\_ \_\_ \_\_\_\_ \_\_ \_\_\_\_ \_\_ \_\_\_ ; seek \_\_\_ \_\_\_ \_\_\_\_ \_\_\_\_ ;
\_\_\_\_\_ \_\_\_ \_\_\_ \_\_\_\_ \_\_\_\_ \_\_ _____ \_\_ \_\_\_ .
Matthew 7:7

**But** _____ \_\_\_ hope \_\_ \_\_\_ _____ \_\_\_\_ renew _____
_____ . \_\_\_\_ \_\_\_ \_\_\_\_ \_\_ \_\_\_\_\_ \_\_\_\_ eagles; \_\_\_\_\_
\_\_\_ \_\_\_ \_\_\_ \_\_\_ \_\_\_\_ \_\_\_\_\_ ; \_\_\_\_ \_\_\_\_ \_\_\_\_ \_\_\_
\_\_\_ \_\_ \_\_\_\_ .
Isaiah 40:31

**Consider** \_\_ \_\_\_\_ \_\_\_ , \_\_ _____ , \_\_\_\_ \_\_\_ experience
trials \_\_ \_\_\_\_\_ \_\_\_\_ , _____ \_\_\_ \_\_\_\_ \_\_\_ _____
\_\_ \_\_\_\_ \_\_\_\_\_ _____ _____ .
James 1:2

**Do** ____ fear, ____ _ _____ **redeemed** ____; _ _____ _____ ____ __ name; ____ ____ _____.
Isaiah 43:1

*I lift* __ __ **eyes** __ ___ _____-_____ ____ __ help ____ ____? __ *help* _____ __ __ ____, ___ Maker __ _____ __ ____.
Psalm 121:1

**Faith** _____ _____ hearing ____ _____, ____ ____ message __ _____ _____ ____ ____ __ _____.
Romans 10:17

**God** _____ ___ ___ love ___ _____ _ __: _____ __ _____ _____ sinners _____ _____ ___ ___.
Romans 5:8

*In* **him** ___ _____ ____ __ **him,** __ ___ *approach God* ____ _____ __ _____.
Ephesians 3:12

**I** ____ __ ___ _____ through Christ ____ _____ __.
Philippians 4:13 NKJV

**Join** __ __ __ _____ __ *praying* __ ___ ___ _.
Romans 15:30

**Know** ____ __ ___ , __ __ *God;* __ _ _ ___ ___ *made* __ __ __ _ _____.
Psalm 100: 3 NKJV

**Live** __ *faith,* ___ __ _____.
2 Corinthians 5:7

**My** ___ ___ *rest* __ ___ ____; __ _____ *comes* ____ ___.
Psalm 62:1

**Now** ____ __ __ *assurance* __ _____ ____ ___, ___ *conviction*
__ _____ __ ___.
Hebrews 11:1 NASB)

*The* **only** ___ ___ *counts* __ ____ *expressing itself* _____ ___.
Galatians 5:6

**Pray** _____.
1 Thessalonians 5:17

*You* **quarrel** __ ____. ___ *do not have* _____ __ __ *not*
___ ___.
James 4:2

*The* **righteous** ___ *live* __ ____.
Romans 1:17

*But David* ____ **strength** __ ___ ___ __ ___.
1 Samuel 30:6

**Trust** __ __ ___ ___ __ ___ *heart* __ *lean* __ __ ___ __
_____ ;__ ___ ___ ___ *acknowledge* ___ , __ __ ___
___ ___ ___ _____.
Proverbs 3:5–6

*I* __ _____; *Help* __ _____ __ **unbelief!**
Mark 9:24

*This* __ ___ **victory** ___ __ *overcome* ___ ____, *even* ___ ____.
1 John 5:4

**Without**_____ __ __ _____ __ *please*___ , _____ _____
__ _____ __ __ ___ _____ __ _____ __ *rewards*_____
__ _____ *seek*___.
Hebrews 11:6

**E(x)cel**__ *everything*, __ _____ , __ _____ , __ _____ , __
complete *earnestness*, ___ __ ____ *love.*
2 Corinthians 8:7

**Yea,** _____ _ *walk* _____ ___ *valley*__ ___ _____ __ ____ , _ ____
*fear no evil,* ___ ___ ____ ____ __.
Psalm 23: 4 NKJV

*The* **zeal**__ ___ ___ _____ ____ *accomplish*____.
Isaiah 37:32

~

## WITNESSING MEMORY VERSES SELF-QUIZ

**All** ____ _____ ____ ____*short* __ ___ _____ __ ___.
Romans 3:23

**Be** _____, _____ , __ ____ *heavenly* _____ __ _____.
Matthew 5:48

**Come**__ __, __ ___ ___ *weary* ___ _____, __ _ ____ ___ __
*rest.*
Matthew 11:28

*You believe* ____ _____ __ __ ___ *God.* ____ ! ____ ___**demons**
_____ __ -___ _____.
James 2:19

___ *gift*__ ___ __ **eternal** ____ *through* _____ _____ ___ ____.
Romans 6:23

**For** __ __ __ *grace* ___ ___ ____ ____ , _____ _____ , ___ ___
__ ____ _____ , __ __ _ ___ ___ , ___ __ ____ ¯ __
___ __ ___ __ ____ .
Ephesians 2:8

**God** __ _____ __ ____ ____ __ *gave* ___ __ ___ ___ ____ ,
___ _____ *believes* __ __ ____ ___ ____ , ___ ___ _____
____.
John 3:16

**He** _____ *bore* ___ ____ __ __ ___ __ ___ _*tree* , __ __
____ __ __ __ ___ __ __ _____; __ ___ *wounds* __ __
____ ____.
1 Peter 2:24

**It** *is* _____.
John 19:30

**Jesus** _____ , "__ *work*__ ___ __ ___: __ *believe* __ ___ __
__ ___ ___".
John 6:39

*All* ___ ____ **know** ____ __ ___ *my disciples if*___ ____ __
_____.
John 13:35

*Thomas* ___ __ __ "__ **Lord** ___ __ __!"
John 20:28

**Now** ___ __ eternal ____: ___ ___ ___ know you, ___ ___ ___
___ , ___ ___ ___ ___ , ___ ___ ___ sent.
John 17:3


*Believe* **on** ___ ___ ___ ___ , ___ ___ ___ __ saved.
Acts 16:31 NKJV


*I* __ ___ ashamed __ ___ gospel , _____ __ __ __ **power** __ __
___ ___ _____ __ _____ ___ believes.
Romans 1:16


*For* _____ ___ creation __ ___ world ___' _____ **qualities-**
___ eternal power ___ divine _____-___ ___ clearly ___ ,
being understood __ ___ ___ ___ made , __ ___ ___ ___ without
_____.
Romans 1:20


*As far* __ ___ east __ ___ ___ west , __ ___ ___ __ **removed** ___
_____ from __.
Psalm 103:12


*That if* ___ confess ___ ___ ___ , " ___ __ ___ " , ___
believe __ ___ ___ ___ raised ___ ___ ___ ___ , ___
___ __ **saved.**
Romans 10:9


*I* _____ **these** _____ __ ___ believe __ ___ name __ ___ ___
__ ___ so that ___ __ know ___ ___ ___ eternal ___.
1 John 5:13


*The* ___ became _____ __ lived ___ _ ____ ____ us.
John 1:14

*I stand* __ __ __ __ *knock.* __ ____ ____ __ **voice** __
*opens* __ __ , _ ____ __ __ ___ *eat* ___ __ , __ _ ___ __.
Revelation 3:20

**We** __ , ___ *sheep,* ___ ___ ____ , __ __ __ ___ *turned* __
___ __ *way;* __ __ __ __ *laid* __ __ __ ____ __
__ __.
Isaiah 53:6

*Set* __ **e(x)ample** __ __ *believers* __ _____ , __ ___ , __ *love,* __
____ __ __ ____.
1 Timothy 4:12

**Yet** __ __ __ *received* __ , __ ____ __ *believed* __ ___ ___ , __
___ __ ____ __ ____ *children* __ __.
John 1:12

*Never* __ _____ __ **zeal,** ___ ___ ___ *spiritual* ____ , *serving*
__ __.
Romans 12:11

⁓

# Worship Memory Verses Self-quiz

**As** ___ ___ *pants* ___ _____ __ ____ , __ __ *soul* ____
___ ___ , _ __.
Psalm 42:1

**Be** ___ , __ *know* ___ _ *am* __.
Psalm 46:10

**Come,** ___ _ sing ___ ___ __ ___ ___; ___ __ shout ____ __
___ Rock__ ___ _____.
Psalm 95:1

*This* __ ___ **day** ___ __ ___ _ made, ___ __ rejoice ___ __ ____
__ __.
Psalm 118:24

*His* ____ **endures** _____.
Psalm 36:7

*Let* __ **fix** ___ *eyes* __ ____, __ ____ __ _____ __ ___ *faith.*
Hebrews 12:2

*Ascribe* _ ___ ____ ___ **glory** ___ ___ *name.*
Psalm 29:2

**How** ____ __ ____ __ *Father* ___ *lavished* __ __ , ___ __ ____
__ ____ ___ *children* __ ___. ___ ___ *is* ___ __ ___.
1 John 3:1

**If** __ *confess* ___ ____, __ __ *faithful* ___ ____ __ ___ *forgive* __
___ ___ ___ *cleanse* __ ____ __ _____.
1 John 1:9

*Through* **Jesus,** _____, ___ __ _____ *offer* __ ___ _
*sacrifice* __ _____ - ___ ____ __ *lips* ___ __ _____ __ ___.
Hebrews 13:15

Your **kingdom** __ __ everlasting _____ ___ ___ _____
endures _____ ___ _____.
Psalm 145:13

*The* **LORD** __ *gracious* ___ _____, ___ __ ____ __
*rich* __ ____.
Psalm 145:8

*God* __ _____ , ___ ____ *worshippers* **must** _____ __ **spirit**
___ __ _____ .
John 4:24

*Let* __ **not** ___ __ *meeting* _____ , __ *some* ___ __ ___ *habit* __
_____.
Hebrews 10:25

**O**, LORD, ___ ____, ___ *majestic* __ ____ *name* __ ___ __ ____ !
Psalm 8:1

**Praise** __ __ __ *God* ___ *Father* __ *our* ____ ____ ____ !
1 Peter 1:4

*Come* ____ _ __ *yourselves* __ _ **quiet** ____ __ __ ___ *rest.*
Mark 6:31

What __ ___ have ____ ___ ___ ___ **receive?**
1 Corinthians 4:7

**Sing** __ ___ LORD _ *new* ____.
Psalm 96:1

**This** __ *love:* ___ ____ __ ____ __ , __ ___ __ ____ __ __
*sent* ___ ____ __ __ *atoning* _____ __ __ *sins.*
1 John 4:10

*Have mercy* __ __ , _ ___ , *according* __ ____ **unfailing** ___.
Psalm 51:1

*Therefore,* _ ____ ___ ,_____ , __ **view** __ ____ - _____ __ *offer*
*your bodies* __ _____ _____ .
Romans 12:1

**Where** ___ __ _____ *come together* __ __ ____, _____ _ __ ____
___.
Matthew 18:20

*Be* **e(x)alted** _ ___, _____ ___ *heavens;* ___ ___ _____ __ ____
___ __ ____.
Psalm 57:5

**You** ___ _ *chosen generation,* _ _____ _____ , _ __ ___ , _
_____ *belonging* __ ___ , ____ ___ ___ *declare* ___ _____ __ __
___ *called* ___ ___ __ *darkness* ____ ___ *marvelous* _____.
1 Peter 2:9

**Zeal** ___ ____ *house* ____ *consume* __.
John 2:17

# ABOUT THE AUTHOR

Herb Ruby grew up in Westminster, Maryland, and after college, he taught and coached high school until sensing a call to gospel ministry. After receiving a Master of Divinity degree from Covenant Theological Seminary in St. Louis, Missouri, he returned to Maryland and planted a church in Reisterstown, Covenant of Grace Presbyterian Church (PCA).

He served as Senior Pastor for thirty-nine years and now serves as Pastor Emeritus. He holds a Doctor of Ministry degree from Westminster Theological Seminary and has served on the faculty of Metro Baltimore Seminary. He has been married to his wife, Shelley, since 1968 and has (at the time of this writing) three married sons, eight grandchildren, and one great-granddaughter.

Made in the USA
Middletown, DE
30 December 2024

68478369R00166